MEDIUM ÆVUM MONOGRAPHS
NEW SERIES IX

DITIÉ DE JEHANNE D'ARC

CHRISTINE DE PISAN

Edited by

ANGUS J. KENNEDY and KENNETH VARTY

Published by the Society for the
Study of Mediæval Languages and Literature
Oxford

THE SOCIETY FOR THE STUDY OF MEDIEVAL
LANGUAGES AND LITERATURE
OXFORD

http://aevum.space/monographs

ISBN-13:
978-0-907570-05-9 (pb)
978-0-907570-49-3 (ebk)

British Library Cataloguing in Publication Data
A catalogue record for this book is available from
the British Library

First published 1977
Reprinted 2003
This reprint, with additional note, first issued 2019

PREFACE

It is hoped that the present edition will be of interest and use to three main groups of readers. Our object has been to make available a critical edition of the *Ditié de Jehanne d'Arc* to Christine de Pisan specialists, to undergraduate students studying French poetry of the later Middle Ages, and to historians interested in the literature of the Hundred Years' War.

We should like to gratefully record our thanks to the many colleagues at Glasgow University and elsewhere who have helped us in our work. Special mention must be made of Professor Lewis Thorpe who encouraged us in our work from its inception and published in *Nottingham Mediaeval Studies* Vol.XVIII (1974) and Vol.XIX (1975) two preparatory articles which form the basis of our edition. We must acknowledge too his kind permission for us to make use of these two articles in the present work.

We (and our readers) owe a special debt to Professor T.B.W. Reid who read our work in typescript and generously sent us his invaluable comments and suggestions on the establishment of the text.

Our thanks are due also to Professor Brian Woledge, Professor James C. Laidlaw and Mr. Michael Bath for the interest which they have shown in our work and for taking time (in the midst of more pressing commitments) to send us their suggestions, or to reply to our queries.

We gratefully acknowledge the help which we have received from the Libraries of Berne, Carpentras and Grenoble; we are grateful in particular for the readiness with which they supplied us with copies of the respective manuscripts of the *Ditié*.

Finally, we must record our gratitude to the Publications Board of the University of Glasgow, the Carnegie Trust for the Universities of Scotland and the British Academy for their generous help in financing the publication of this edition.

Note to the 2019 Reprint

Pisan or Pizan

This edition is of its time. Up until the 1970s 'Pisan' was the standard form of Christine's surname. The subsequent identification of Christine's autograph manuscripts (in which her surname is given as 'Pizan') explains the switch from -s to the correct form with -z used today. The form 'Pizan' has the additional advantage of linking Christine's origins with Pizzano (and not Pisa).

A. J. K. and K. V.

TABLE OF CONTENTS

INTRODUCTION

As the first poem to have been composed – in any language – on Joan of Arc,[1] the only major one to have been written while Joan was still alive, and the last from the pen of a distinguished poetess, the *Ditié de Jehanne d'Arc* has unique claims to fame. The extrinsic value of the *Ditié* as an historical document is self-evident. It was completed on 31 July 1429, in the midst of continuing successes on the part of the French army which had just taken Château-Thierry, on 29 July. With the brilliant victory at Orléans and the coronation at Rheims now behind them, Joan and Charles VII were expected to enter Paris at any moment, defeat the Anglo-Burgundian forces and thus bring to an end the long years of foreign occupation and civil strife. What gives Christine's poem its unique 'documentary' value is the fact that it vividly captures not only the surge of optimism and triumph that swept through the whole of the French camp at this time, but also the sense of wonder and gratitude which all loyal Frenchmen must have felt at the miraculous intervention of divine Providence in the person of Joan. Yet important as the poem's historical interest undoubtedly is, the *Ditié* merits attention for a number of other reasons which previous editors have either ignored or only touched upon in passing: the *Ditié* deserves to be studied as a literary and linguistic document in its own right, and also for the light it has to shed on Christine's literary career as a whole. It has been our main aim to make available a critical edition of the poem which attempts to do justice to these rather neglected areas of interest; at the same time, we have tried to give due weight to the undeniable historical, documentary value of the *Ditié* by including a plain prose translation into English which, it is hoped, will make an often difficult and obscure poem more easily accessible to readers who are not themselves Middle French specialists.

Date and Place of Composition

The *Ditié de Jehanne d'Arc* is Christine's last surviving work and, with the possible exception of the *Heures de Contemplacion sur la Passion de Nostre Seigneur* (tentatively dated 1420 by S. Solente[2]) the only one known to have been written during the years of Christine's enforced exile from Paris, from 1418 till 1430, the probable date of her death. Much of the detail relating to the composition of the *Ditié* can be deduced directly from internal evidence, or by relating the poem both to Christine's previous life and work and to the well-documented career of Joan of Arc. The first and final *huitains* indicate that the poem was completed on 31 July 1429, in the 'abbaye close' where Christine had lived for the preceding eleven years (see l.2) i.e. since 1418, when the arrival of the Burgundian troops in Paris had forced her and many others to flee and seek protection outside the city. Although there is no conclusive evidence available, it is likely that the 'abbaye close' referred to was the royal abbey of Dominicans at Poissy, where Christine's only daughter had taken orders c. 1396.[3] That Christine may have found refuge there is suggested by a marginal note in the fifteenth-century *Boke of Noblesse* (British Museum, Royal 18 B XXII) inserted by William Worcester, secretary to Sir John Fastolf: 'Notandum est quod Cristina fuit domina praeclara natu et moribus et manebat in domo religiosarum dominarum apud Passye prope Parys... et vixit circa annum Christi 1430, sed floruit ab anno Christi 1400.'[4] As for the date on which she began the poem, this can be deduced in approximate terms from the references in the *Ditié* to Joan's and Charles' achievements: ll. 225–8 refer to Joan's journey (from Vaucouleurs to Chinon) and her reception by the Dauphin (February–March 1429), ll. 229–240 to the interrogation to which Joan had been subjected at Poitiers (March–April), ll. 257–64 to the raising of the siege at Orléans (8 May), ll. 377–84 to the coronation at Rheims (17 July), ll. 391–3 to their stay in and departure from that city (21 July), ll. 394–448 to their triumphant entry into a number of towns and cities during their expected advance on Paris (Charles and Joan were at Vailly on 22 July, at Soissons from 23 to 28 July, at Château-Thierry on 29 July). While it is conceivable that at least part of the *Ditié* may have been drafted shortly after the raising of the siege of Orléans,[5] these details would suggest rather that the greater part of the poem was composed in a very short period of time, between, say, 23 and and 31 July 1429.[6]

Manuscripts of the Poem

Two complete fifteenth-century manuscript versions of the poem are known, and one incomplete version which could be from the late fifteenth century but is more likely to be from the sixteenth century.

1. *The Berne manuscript.* Berne 205 was first mentioned by J.R. Sinner in his *Catalogus codicum mss bibliothecae Bernensis*, Berne, 1760–72. It is described in detail in H. Hagen's *Catalogus codicum Bernensium (Bibliotheca Bongarsiana)*, Berne, Haller, 1874, pp. 248–54, and in the edition of the *Ditié de Jehanne d'Arc* published by Ch. de Roche and G. Wissler in the *Festschrift Louis Gauchat*, Aarau, 1926, pp. 330–332; a briefer description will be found in the *Rapport à M. le Ministre de l'Instruction Publique*, Paris, A La Librairie Spéciale des Sociétés Savantes, 1838, pp. 15–6, 22, published by Achille Jubinal, who first brought Christine's poem to

light in 1838. Berne 205 originally contained 570ff., but a number of leaves have now been lost and others bound out of sequence: ff. 1–6, 83–102, 127, 167–8, 201, 324–64, 393, 395–412, 414–519, 547–50 are missing; ff. 156–66 follow f. 376 and f. 394 follows f. 413. The *Ditié de Jehanne d'Arc* is the fourteenth item of 165 different entries (following Hagen's classification) and occupies ff. 62^{r}–68^{r}.

The contents of Berne 205, written partly in French, partly in Latin, vary enormously in length and subject-matter. The entries do not seem to have been arranged in any special order, serious items relating to law, science, grammar, theology, medicine and literature being freely intermingled with light-hearted or satirical matter. Of particular interest are a number of items concerning Joan of Arc: in addition to the *Ditié* and immediately following it are the *Lettres closes envoiées de par la pucelle au roy d'Angleterre* (22 March 1429) and the *Consultation de Poitiers* (March-April 1429) ff. 68^{r}–69^{r}, and, as item 44, ff. 133^{r}–133^{v}, *Versus XVI in Johannam d'Arc.* De Roche and Wissler have drawn attention[7] to the fact that the main documents on Joan (the *Ditié*, the *Lettres closes* and the *Consultation de Poitiers*) are grouped together and immediately preceded in the manuscript by the credentials of one of the compilers of Berne 205, Nicolas du Pleissy, who was nominated 'procureur du bailliage et garde des sceaux de la prévôté de Sens' on 17 January 1430, no doubt as a reward for his loyalty to Charles VII. Given that Nicolas must have begun his compilation c. 1428 (the note on f. 257 recording the birth of his first son Guiot was entered on 13 July 1428), it is likely that the entries on Joan were made shortly after the dates to which they refer. If this is so, it is clear that Berne 205 contains what must have been one of the earliest copies made of Christine's *Ditié de Jehanne d'Arc.*

As the photographic reproduction of the *Ditié* shows, the poem appears to have been copied by one hand, though there is evidence of changes of pen possibly coinciding with different copying-sessions (see Plate VI and compare the first three *huitains* on the right with the last two). With the exception of f. 62^{v} (which contains two *huitains*) and f. 68^{r} (which contains four *huitains*), there are five *huitains* per side. Though the manuscript is relatively neatly executed, the scribe made a number of self-corrections and alterations (see e.g. Plate II, last line of fourth *huitain* on right) and clearly had difficulty in understanding parts of the manuscript from which he was copying (see e.g. Plate II, fourth line of second *huitain* on right); in addition, he made a number of slips, particularly in the latter sections of the poem. It is evident, therefore, that while Berne 205 probably represents the oldest version of the *Ditié* to have survived, the text which it contains requires on occasion to be corrected in the light of the other manuscripts.

2. *The Carpentras manuscript.* The *Ditié* occupies ff. 81r–90v of MS. 390 in the Bibliothèque Inguimbertine at Carpentras. This manuscript, which does not seem to have been known to the nineteenth-century editors of the poem, is described in C.G.A. Lambert's *Catalogue descriptif et raisonné des manuscrits de la bibliothèque de Carpentras*, Carpentras, E. Rolland, tome 1, 1862, pp. 218–221; in M. Duhamel's *Catalogue général des manuscrits des bibliothèques publiques de France. Départements*, Tome XXXIV: *Carpentras*, Plon, tome 1, 1901, pp. 193–5; and in J. C. Laidlaw's *The Poetical Works of Alain Chartier*, Cambridge University Press, 1974, p. 120. Carpentras 390 is a fifteenth-century, leather-bound, paper manuscript which measures 305 × 220 mm; it contains 79ff. numbered 11–39, 41–90 and is made up of an anthology of poems of which Christine's *Ditié* is the last: *Le Psautier des Vilains* ff. 11–20, *l'Hospital d'Amours* ff. 21–37, *La Belle Dame sans Mercy* ff. 38–55, *l'Excusacion aux Dames* ff. 55–60, *Debat de l'amant et de la dame* ff. 61–68, a *pastourelle* ff. 69–72, *Debat de Reveille Matin* ff. 73–80, *Ditié de Jehanne d'Arc* ff. 81r–90v. Little is known of the history of the manuscript apart from the fact that it once belonged to a de Castellane family, whose names occur frequently in the text – immediately after the Explicit of the *Ditié*, for example, there is the signature of Henry de Castellane.

Christine's *Ditié* is neatly written out, 25 lines to a side, with no spacing between the *huitains*. Thus, f. 81v begins with *huitain* IV, line 2, 82r with VII, line 3, 82v with X, line 4 etc; for an illustration of f. 88v *huitain* XLVIII, lines 2–8 to *huitain* LI, lines 1–3, see Plate VIIIb. The *huitains* are distinguished from each other by a small marginal letter placed usually about 1–2 cms. to the left of the first word of each *huitain*. For example, on f. 82r the letters *o*, *e* and *q* are written in the margin, indicating the initial words of VIII, IX and X respectively. As for the date of this transcription, it is impossible to be more specific than 'fifteenth-century'; it is unlikely, however, that Carpentras 390 could be earlier than Berne 205.

3. *The Grenoble manuscript.* An important fragment of the *Ditié* is kept in the Bibliothèque Municipale de Grenoble, where it forms part of Ms. U. 909. Rés., the *Registre Delphinal*. A description of this manuscript will be found in the *Catalogue général des manuscrits des bibliothèques publiques de France. Départements*. Tome VII: *Grenoble*, by P. Fournier, E. Maignien, and A. Prudhomme, Plon, 1889, pp. 314–6. The manuscript is of vellum and paper, measures 300 × 205 mm. and is dated fifteenth-sixteenth century. It was lent to the Bibliothèque Municipale de Grenoble by Berriat-Saint-Prix in 1820 and bequeathed to the same library in 1836.

The *Registre Delphinal* was the work of Matthieu Thomassin who had been commissioned by the Dauphin Louis, the future Louis XI, on 20 May 1456, to collect documents relating to 'les droiz, fais, gestes et choses du Dauphiné'. Thomassin claims that his collection is divided into three parts: the first of these was to deal with the Kingdom of Vienne and Burgundy, the second was to relate 'comment la dignité dalphinale fut mise sus après la fin dudit royaulme', while the third was to deal with 'la translation du Dauphiné à la maison de France.' In fact, Thomassin often assembles his material at random and does not really adhere to this classification. The *Ditié* is found within part 1 which extends as far as f. 117, and occupies ff. 98–102.

When Thomassin comes to write about Joan of Arc and Christine, he does so with great feeling, stressing the way in which each may be considered to have brought honour to the female sex: 'Mais sur tous les signes d'amour que Dieu a envoyez au Royaulme il n'y a point eu de si grand ne de si merveilleux comme de ceste pucelle. Et pour ce grandes croniques en sont faictes. Et entre les autres une notable femme appellée Christine qui a faict plusieurs livres en françoys (je l'ay souvent veue à Paris) fist de l'advenement de ladite pucelle et de ses gestes ung traictié dont je mectray cy seulement le plus special touchant ladicte pucelle. Et ay lessé le demourant, car ce seroit trop long à mectre icy. Et j'ay plustost desiré de mectre icy le traictié de ladite Christine que des autres affin de tousjours honnorer le sexe feminin par le moyen duquel toute chrestienté a eu tant de biens – par la pucelle vierge Marie, la reparacion et restauracion de tout le humain lignaige; et par ladicte pucelle Jehanne, la reparacion et restauracion du royaume de France qui estoit du tout en bas, jusques à prendre fin, si ne fust venue. Pour ce bien doit de chacun estre louée, combien que les angloys et les alliez en ont dit tous les maulx qu'ilz ont peu dire; mais les faictz de laditte pucelle les ont rendus et rendent tous mensongers et confus' (ff. 97v–98r).

Thomassin then begins to quote from the *Ditié*, beginning with *huitain* XX 'Ah! soyes loué, hault Dieu!', continuing with XXI–XXXIV, XXXVI, XXXIX–XLI, XXXV, and ending with XLIV–LII, i.e. quoting 29 *huitains* altogether. These extracts begin on f. 98r and extend to the bottom of f. 102r; no attempt is made to copy the same number of lines per page (this varies from 22 to 28), nor to begin a *huitain* at the top or to end one at the bottom of a page. The handwriting, in black ink, is very neat and all apparently by the same scribe. The initial letter of each *huitain* is coloured, and the remainder of the first word or words of XX–XXIII is in large black lettering. As indicated above, the compilation of the contents of the Grenoble manuscript was not begun until after 20 May 1456, but presumably soon after. It is likely, however, that Grenoble U.909. Rés. is a late fifteenth- or sixteenth-century copy of Thomassin's compilation.

Relationship of the manuscripts. No obvious relationship between the three manuscripts is evident to us. As the variants and notes to the text show, they differ from each other on the content of the *Ditié* in only relatively minor ways, but such variation as there is makes it clear that they are all probably independent of each other.

Previous Editions

Several complete or partial editions of the *Ditié* appeared in the nineteenth century, and there has been one complete one in the twentieth. None of the nineteenth-century editors knew of the Carpentras manuscript, which was first used by de Roche and Wissler in their edition of the poem published in 1926.

1. Achille Jubinal, 'Ung Beau Ditié fait par Christine de Pisan à la louange de Jeanne d'Arc' in *Rapport à M. le Ministre de l'Instruction publique, suivi de quelques pièces inédites tirées des manuscrits de la Bibliothèque de Berne,* Paris, A la Librairie Spéciale des Sociétés Savantes, 1838, pp. 75–88.

This edition contains the first transcription of all 61 *huitains* of the Berne manuscript which Jubinal brought to light during the survey which he made of the Berne Library on behalf of the Ministre de l'Instruction publique. Misreadings of the manuscript are numerous, some of these resulting from Jubinal's failure to recognise scribal abbreviations (e.g. he prints *Chrispine* for *Christine* l.1, *guerre* for *grace* l.88, *soit* for *seroit* l.114, *Charles* for *faite* l.458); emendations are frequently made but not indicated (e.g. ll. 24 and 55); the orthography has been unnecessarily modernised (e.g. *toujours* for *tousjours* l.3, *merci* for *mercy* l.30, *lys* for *lix* l.96) and the punctuation is often open to question (e.g. ll.145–7, 216), There is no critical apparatus, and no reference is made to the Grenoble fragment which was published in the same year by Buchon.

2. J.A.C. Buchon, 'Documents divers sur Jeanne d'Arc' in *Choix de chroniques et mémoires sur l'histoire de France avec notes et notices,* vol. XXXIV of the *Panthéon Littéraire,* Paris, Desrez, 1838, pp. 540–3.

This edition contains the first and only transcription to date of the fragment of the *Ditié* in the *Registre Delphinal,* but is unfortunately full of inaccuracies, many of them serious (compare, for example, Buchon's transcription of *huitain* XXI with the original text as it is found in the Grenoble manuscript, f.98r). There is no critical apparatus apart from eleven footnotes which contain Buchon's modern French equivalents of words or phrases in the text.

3. Raymond Thomassy, *Essai sur les écrits politiques de Christine de Pisan,* Paris, Debécourt, 1838. On pp. XLII–XLVII of his introduction, Thomassy prints a selection of *huitains*: I, first four lines of III and last four of XI printed as one *huitain,* XIII, XVIII, XXI, XXIV, XXXIV, XXXV, XXXVI, XLII, XLIII, XXXIX, XLVI, XLVII, XLVIII, LXI. This is an unreliable transcription, the material for which Thomassy received from Jubinal, before the latter's publication of the poem.

4. Jules Quicherat, 'Christine de Pisan' in the section entitled 'Témoignages des Poëtes du XVe siècle' in *Procès de condamnation et de réhabilitation de Jeanne d'Arc dite la Pucelle,* vol. V, Paris, Renouard, 1849, pp. 3–21.

The inclusion of Christine's poem in Quicherat's great pioneering work on Joan of Arc ensured that his became the most widely-known version of the *Ditié.* Yet important and valuable as this edition is, it has a number of serious deficiencies. Although Quicherat states that he will reproduce 'le texte de la pièce tout entière, telle que M. Jubinal l'a publiée en 1838 d'après le manuscrit de Berne', this is not in fact what he does. While basing himself on Jubinal (and therefore reproducing the bulk of Jubinal's errors), he makes extensive and often unacknowledged use of Buchon's completely unreliable transcription of the Grenoble fragment. Consequently, unless the reader has access to the printed editions of Jubinal and Buchon, it is impossible to follow the method by which Quicherat established his composite text.

5. H. Herluison, *Jeanne d'Arc; Chronique Rimée par Christine de Pisan,* Orléans, Herluison, 1865, pp. 41.

This attractive little text (its pages measure only 11 × 7 cms.) was published in a limited edition of 100 copies. The text is based on Quicherat and therefore reproduces Quicherat's errors. Differences between Quicherat and Herluison are minor, and probably result from misprints or from the latter's instinctive modernisation of spelling.

6. Le Roux de Lincy et L. M. Tisserand, 'Apostrophe de Christine de Pisan aux Parisiens dans "Ung Beau Ditié fait l'an M. CCCC. XXIX" à la louange de Jeanne d'Arc', in *Paris et ses historiens,* Paris, Imprimerie Impériale, 1867, pp. 420–7.

This is an incomplete edition, or rather a selection of 38 of the poem's 61 *huitains*: I–VI, XIII–XIV, XXI–XXV, XXVII–XXX, XXXIII–XXXVI, XXXIX–XLV, XLVIII–LI, LIII–LVI and LX–LXI. The text is based on Jubinal and therefore reproduces Jubinal's errors. Differences between Le Roux de Lincy/Tisserand and Jubinal are minor, and are concerned for the most part with punctuation, distribution of accents and modernisation of spelling.

7. Joseph-Amant Fabre, 'Stances de Christine de Pisan sur Jeanne d'Arc' in *Procès de réhabilitation de Jeanne d'Arc*, 1888, republished Paris, Hachette, 1913, tome 2, pp.307–330.

Fabre has reproduced, with minor modifications, the Quicherat edition; in addition, immediately after words or expressions likely to be unfamiliar to his readers, he has printed what he considers to be their modern French equivalent.

The relationship of the nineteenth-century editions to the manuscripts and to each other may be summed up diagrammatically in the following way:

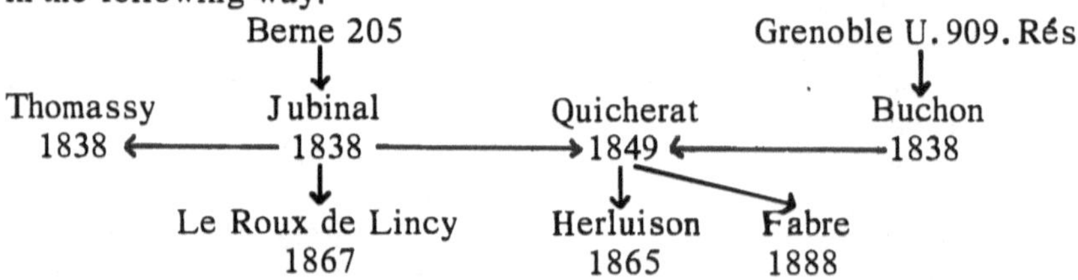

8. Ch. de Roche and G. Wissler, 'Documents relatifs à Jeanne d'Arc et à son époque extraits d'un manuscrit du XVe siècle de la Bibliothèque de la ville de Berne' in *Festschrift Louis Gauchat,* Aarau, 1926, pp. 329–52.

This represents the first attempt at a critical edition of the poem, based as it is on all three known manuscripts (Berne, Carpentras and Grenoble). It forms part of a study/edition of all the documents in Berne 205 relating to Joan of Arc. There is a valuable description of the base manuscript, Berne 205, pp. 330–2, a brief discussion of the poem pp.332–3 and a short account of the Grenoble and Carpentras manuscripts p.334; the poem then follows on pp.335–50, with variants at the foot of each page; there are two pages of explanatory notes at the end, pp.351–2.

Although this is by far the most valuable of all the previous editions of the poem, it has nonetheless a number of serious disadvantages: there are many misreadings (e.g. *vugle* for *bugle* l.371) unnecessary rejections of the base manuscript Berne 205 (e.g. l.216), and modernisations of orthography (e.g. l.101, 103); emendations are made without an indication of this always being given (e.g. l.364); the variants are not complete and contain in any case a number of errors (e.g. the reading *voire* does not occur in Carpentras l.9; l.197 is not omitted from the Berne manuscript); unless he has direct access to the manuscripts, the reader cannot tell whether the text has been established (a) in the light of the editors' 'common-sense' emendation or (b) in the light of a manuscript reading; finally, there is no glossary or notes on points of linguistic interest or difficulty.

The present edition

We have decided to use Berne 205 as our base manuscript on the grounds that it probably represents the oldest surviving version of the *Ditié*. Nonetheless, Berne 205 does not deserve unqualified respect since it contains, as we have indicated, a number of scribal errors and misunderstandings. For the most part, these have been corrected in the light of the corresponding readings in Carpentras 390 or, if applicable, Grenoble U. 909. Rés. The latter has been found most useful in establishing the text of *huitain* XLIX. Hypometric and hypermetric lines in Berne 205 have been corrected to lines of eight syllables, usually in the light of the other manuscripts. We have resolved scribal abbreviations, distinguished between i and j, u and v, introduced punctuation and capital letters and distributed a limited number of accents. All words or letters added to Berne 205 (whether they occur in the other two manuscripts or not) have been printed in square brackets. Two additional minor modifications have been made: (i) the scribe's spelling of the indefinite subject pronoun *on* alternates between *on* and *en*. We have regularised this usage throughout in favour of *on*, in order to avoid confusion with modern French *en*. (ii) Where appropriate we have used the apostrophe to indicate elision e. g. since *que aucuns* l.485 is equal to two syllables, we print this as *qu'aucuns*. All such modifications have been indicated. A full list of variants from Carpentras 390 and Grenoble U. 909. Rés. appears in Section I of the Notes; readings in the base manuscript, Berne 205, which have been rejected, and all our comments, are printed in this section in italics. Section II of the Notes contains comments on points of literary, historical and linguistic interest. A glossary will be found on pp. 81–101.

Structure and Themes

Although there are grounds for believing, as has been seen, that the *Ditié* was hastily composed, it has nonetheless a clearly-defined and logical structure which betrays a conscious effort on Christine's part to organise her material into a coherent, unified whole. After a brief introductory section (*huitains* I–XII) in which she states that it is her main intention to relate how God brought back the sun and spring into her own life by miraculously restoring the fortunes of France and the French Crown (see ll.49–50: 'Mais or vueil raconter comment/ Dieu a tout ce fait de sa grace...') Christine deals in turn with Charles VII (XIII–XX), Joan of Arc (XXI–XXXVI), the French troops (XXXVII–XXXVIII), France's enemies i.e. the English (XXXIX–XLI, XLV)[8] and their allies (the Burgundians, Paris, 'toutes villes rebelles', XLVI–LIX). In a concluding section (LX–LXI) Christine states that she is aware that the contents of her poem may well displease some people (see ll.484–488: 'Mais j'entens/ Qu'aucuns se tendront mal contens/ De ce qu'il contient, car qui chiere/ A embrunche, et les yeux pesans,/ Ne puet regarder la lumiere[9]') but prays to God nonetheless that all Frenchmen will assert their loyalty to Charles VII so that France may look forward to a reign of peace and prosperity. When one notes that the poem thus reflects a descending, hierarchical pattern (God–Charles VII–Joan–the French troops–the English and their allies) and, in addition, that Christine has been careful to weave into each section (particularly the central section on Joan herself, XXI–XXXVI) a reminder that what Joan's achievements primarily reveal is the hand of Providence at work (see, for example, ll.171–5, 187–8, 207, 288), it is clear that the structure of the *Ditié* is itself an expression of Christine's main intentions and priorities as they are defined in the opening section i.e. to praise and glorify God for having delivered France from affliction. The same point is further highlighted by a number of parallelisms and contrasts neatly worked into the opening and closing sections of the *Ditié*: the first *huitain* proclaims the joy which Christine experiences on a personal, individual level ('Je Christine . . . / Ore à prime me prens à rire'), while *huitain* LX seems to anticipate the joy in which all Frenchmen may share if they re-assert their allegiance to Charles ('Si pry Dieu qu'Il mecte en courage/ A *vous tous* qu'ainsy le faciez . . . '); the poem opens with a reminder of 'la traïson' (l.7) which had forced both the Dauphin and Christine to flee from Paris in 1418, and closes with Christine summoning all Frenchmen to swear their loyalty to Charles, now about to re-enter Paris as King; and, finally, the mention of 'l'an dessusdit' in l.482, together with the image contained in the very last lines of the poem ('. . . car qui chiere/ A embrunche, et les yeux pesans,/ Ne puet regarder *la lumiere.*'), takes the reader's mind right back to *huitain* III, in which Christine joyfully declares that 'L'an mil CCCCXXIX/ Reprint à luire *li soleil./ . . .* plus de rien je ne me dueil,/ Quant ores *voy* ce que [je] veulx' ll.17–8, 23–4). Much of the detail of the structure, therefore, as well as its general outlines unobtrusively and suggestively points to Christine's central theme, the miraculous intervention of Providence, and the transformation which this has brought about in her own and France's fortunes.

As one traces the development of this theme through the poem, it soon becomes apparent that Christine's response to Joan's achievements is expressed on at least three different levels: as a devout Christian, she is concerned first and foremost (as the overall structure of the poem has already made clear) to express her heart-felt thanks to God for having entrusted Joan with her mission; as a patriot, she pays eloquent tribute to the French victory over the English and their allies, which will, she hopes, put an end to the twin evils of foreign occupation and civil strife, and lay the foundations of peace and political stability in France; and as a life-long defender of the feminist cause, she sees the opportunity to restate her case more tellingly than ever before. Each of these elements, which are developed simultaneously in the poem, will now be examined briefly in turn.

Given that Christine herself had been the author of a number of exclusively devotional works (*L'Oroyson Nostre Dame* c.1402, *Les XV Joyes Nostre Dame, Une Oroyson de Nostre Seigneur,* both before 1408, *Les Sept Psaumes Allegorisés* c.1409 and the *Heures de Contemplacion sur la Passion de Nostre Seigneur* c.1420), and that she had, it will be remembered, spent the preceding eleven years in an 'abbaye close', it was inevitable that in the *Ditié* she should devote most attention to the religious significance of Joan's coming. That she wrote the *Ditié* primarily as a hymn of praise and thanksgiving to God (and intended it to be read as such) is clearly indicated in a number of ways. To begin with, she states in the opening section of the poem that the particular 'example' of Joan is illustrative of a general truth about life, namely, that it is Providence, not capricious Fortune, which ultimately governs all men's destinies (see ll.57–72, and in particular ll.69–72: 'Voie⟨z⟩ comment tousjours n'est une/ Fortune, qui a nuit à maint!/ Car Dieu, qui aux tors faiz repune,/ Ceulx relieve en qui espoir maint!'[10]). She reminds us that it was Providence which had predestined Joan to play her particular role (see, for example, the prophecies mentioned in ll.239–248, 333–4, and *huitains* XLI–XLIII, which predict Joan's future achievements i.e. the complete and final overthrow of the English, the restoration of peace not just in France but in Christendom as a whole, the destruction of heretics and the reconquest of the Holy Land). She links Joan, just as her friend and ally Jean Gerson had done in his treatise *De quadam puella,* written c.March–April 1429 in defence of Joan's divine claims,[11] to a succession of Old Testament heroes and heroines who had themselves lived out their lives as the specially-chosen agents of Providence (ll.179, 193, 209, 217). She lays particular stress on the miraculous nature of Joan's achievement (it is described in l.58 as 'Chose sur toute merveillable', in ll.81,

225, 260 as a 'miracle', in l.192 as a 'chose oultre nature', in 202 as a 'si grant merveille' and in l.274 as 'chose fors nature'). Lastly and most importantly of all, she works into practically every reference to Joan a reminder that her powers originate directly from God: 'Chose est bien digne de memoire/ Que *Dieu*, par une vierge tendre/ Ait adès voulu (chose est voire!)/ Sur France si grant grace estendre' (ll.85–8)... 'Et toy, Pucelle beneurée,/ Y dois-tu estre obliée,/ Puis que *Dieu* t'a tant honnorée' (ll.161–3)... 'Tu, Jehanne, de bonne heure née,/ Benoist soit cil qui te créa!/ Pucelle de *Dieu* ordonnée' (ll.169–172)... 'une jeune pucelle,/ A qui *Dieu* force et povoir donne/ D'estre le champion' (ll.186–8)... 'Mais tout ce fait *Dieu*, qui la menne' (l.288)... 'N'appercevez-vous, gent avugle,/ Que *Dieu* a icy la main mise?' (ll.369–70). It will have been seen from this that the *Ditié* is primarily a religious poem, designed to praise and glorify God for having delivered France from humiliation and suffering; as such it captures the sense of wonder and thankfulness that the whole French camp must have felt at what Joan had already achieved and at what she was expected to achieve in the near future. 'Le miracle de Jeanne', as Marie-Joseph Pinet has pointed out,[12] 'la Providence divine dans le fait de Jeanne, c'est la grande idée inspiratrice du dittié.'

The second level on which the poem ought to be read concerns, as indicated, Christine's response as a patriot to the coming of Joan of Arc.[13] To assess this response in its proper context and perspective it is essential to look briefly at the development of Christine's reaction to and reflections on the war, as formulated in her previous works. The best-known and perhaps most representative of her earliest writings on the subject are the three 'ballades' *Sur le Combat de Sept Français contre Sept Anglais* (19th May 1402)[14] which give militant expression to Christine's passionate attachment to France. In these three poems she extols the valour of the French knights who '...ont occis et mené a oultrance/ L'orgueil anglois', and praises God for thus having furthered the French cause: 'Louez soit Dieux qui de si grans perilz/ Vous a gittez, tant vous a enamez/ Que vous avez desconfiz, mors et pris/ Les sept Anglois de grant orgueil surpris...' Although this militant anti-Englishness will recur in much of Christine's subsequent writings, to find its fullest expression indeed in the *Ditié de Jehanne d'Arc*, it is interesting to note that it is soon matched, at a very early stage, by an ever-growing awareness of the need for peace. Christine's increasing horror at the disruptive effects of war and civil strife, and the inevitable gratuitous violence which they bring in their wake, is reflected in general terms in the *Livre du Chemin de Long Estude* (1403), the *Livre de la Mutacion de Fortune* (1403) and the *Avision-*

Christine (1405)[15], and more specifically in the *Epistre à la Reine* of 5th October 1405 (an appeal to Isabella of Bavaria to settle the differences between the Dukes of Orléans and Burgundy), the *Livre du Corps de Policie* (1407), the *Lamentacion sur les maux de la France* (1410) and the *Livre de la Paix* (c.1413). The following lines from the *Livre de la Paix*[16] can be seen as representative in this respect: 'Tout royaume divisé en soy sera desolé et toute cité ou maison divisée contre le bien de soy meismes ne puet avoir durée'... 'O! quel chose est aujourdhui au monde plus delictable que paix'... 'O Dieux! où est le cuer qui tout ne doye fremir pensant la perilleuse aventure où ce royaume a esté de toute perdicion à cause de ceste piteuse guerre.' What is important to note is that all of these works, as well as expressing her concern for France's plight, also point to what Christine sees as the only practical, long-term solution: at a time when the Church was dissipating its energies either in the conflicts of the Great Schism or in lavish displays of pomp and pageantry, Christine inevitably centres all her hopes on the monarchy, which she sees as the only effective force capable of protecting France against enemies both within and without her frontiers (see, for example, the concluding section of the *Livre du Chemin de Long Estude*, or the chapters on 'le bon prince' in the *Livre du Corps de Policie* and the *Livre de la Paix*, which sketch out a didactic portrait of the ideal ruler based on Christine's admiration for her father's patron, Charles V[17]). When one turns now to the *Ditié de Jehanne d'Arc* and reads it within the context of Christine's political writings as a whole, it soon becomes apparent that her last surviving work blends together all the different elements which characterise her patriotism: her militant anti-Englishness, her sense of total commitment to France and the French Crown, and, above all, her desire to see France enjoy the benefits of lasting peace.

Christine's militant anti-Englishness is most effectively illustrated by *huitains* XXXIII, XXXIV, XXXIX–XLI and XLV, in which she exults in Joan's victory by heaping scorn on the defeated enemy. What is particularly indicative of her fierce sense of national identity is the concrete, violent, abusive nature of the language used in reference to the English (see, for example, ll.305–8: 'Si rabaissez, Anglois, voz cornes/ Car jamais n'aurez beau gibier!/ En France ne menez voz sornes!/ Matez estes en l'eschiquier'; ll.357–60: 'Quant des Anglois, qui que s'en rie/ Ou pleure, il en est sué./ Le temps avenir moquerie/ En sera fait. Jus sont rué!'; ll.267, 271, 315, where the enemy is described respectively as 'ce grant pueple chenin', 'les traictres' and 'faulse mesgnié[e]'; and l.354, where all that they stand for is summed up in the contemptuous, perjorative term 'l'Englecherie'). As well as finding expression in this negative way, Christine's patriotism is directly reflected in her absolute and unshakeable conviction, akin to that of Turold's in the *Chanson de Roland*, that God has espoused the French cause and positively wills the defeat of the enemy (see X and XLI; there is indeed, *mutatis mutandis*, a distinct crusading ring to ll.321–3, both in the language used and the thought expressed: 'Et sachez que par elle Anglois/ Seront mis jus sans relever,/ Car *Dieu le veult*...'); it is further reflected in her equally firm belief that God has singled out the French monarchy for His special regard and affection (see ll.89–92: 'O quel honneur à la couronne/ De France par divine preuve!/ Car par les graces qu'Il lui donne/ Il appert comment Il l'apreuve'), in her discreet attempt to remind the King of the corresponding obligations he has thereby inherited towards the people entrusted to his care (see XVIII and LVIII in which Christine lists all the qualities which she hopes will be embodied in Charles VII,[18] or describes those which already are), in the sense of exaltation which she experiences at the news of the liberation of Orléans and the subsequent recapture of territory that had once been lost (XXXIII, XXXVI, L), in the warmth and pride with which she speaks of the French troops, who will win for themselves not only earthly honour and glory but also a special place in Paradise (XXXVII–VIII), and, perhaps most simply but most eloquently of all, in the instinctive, repeated mention of the word 'France' (ll.34, 77, 88, 90, 121, 134, 149, 165, 189, 244, 281, 307, 313). Christine's attachment to France is expressed finally, as indicated above, in the reassertion of her commitment to peace: in ll.157–160 she expresses her thanks to God 'Par qui nous sommes parvenus/ A *paix*, et hors de grant tempeste!'; in ll.166–8, 185–190 and 351–2, Joan is greeted not just as victor but as the instrument of peace and political stability... 'Te pourroit-on assez louer/ Quant ceste terre, humiliée/ Par guerre, as fait de *paix* douer?' ... 'Considerée ta personne,/ Qui es une jeune pucelle,/ A qui Dieu force et povoir donne/ D'estre le champion et celle/ Qui donne à France la mamelle/ De *paix* et doulce norriture'...'Si croy que Dieu ça jus l'adonne/ Afin que *paix* soit par son fait'; and the poem closes, it will be remembered, with Christine's prayer that all Frenchmen (rebels included) will swear allegiance to Charles VII and thereby bring an end to civil strife: 'Si pry Dieu qu'Il mecte en courage/ A vous tous qu'ainsy le faciez,/ Afin que le cruel orage/ De ces guerres soit effaciez,/ Et que vostre vie passiez/ En *paix*, soubz vostre chief greigneur,/ Si que jamais ne l'offensiez/ Et que vers vous soit bon seigneur.'. When these lines are read in conjunction with *huitain* XVIII, in which she expresses all the hopes she cherishes for Charles VII, it becomes clear that, for Christine, the peace brought about by Joan could best be maintained by a strong but enlightened French monarchy conscious of its obligations towards its subjects. Commitment to the well-being of France thus overlaps completely, for very practical reasons, with commitment to the French Crown. As one of Christine's earliest biographers has rightly pointed out, 'Ce qu'elle a en vue, c'est l'intérêt public... l'intérêt immédiat et pratique de sa patrie d'adoption la France.'[19]

The third level on which the poem may be read concerns Christine's response as a feminist[20] to Joan's achievements. Given Christine's involvement in the so-called 'Débat sur le *Roman de la Rose*' c.1400–02, when, aided by Jean Gerson and Guillaume de Tignonville, she had undertaken the defence of her sex against the strictures of Jean de Meung and his disciples, given, too, her spirited advocacy of the same cause both before and after the debate proper,[21] it is easy to understand the particular sense of triumph she must have felt at the news of Joan's victories. The raising of the siege of Orléans, the coronation of the Dauphin at Rheims, the retreat of the English and their allies – all of this, Christine is careful to point out, had been made possible by a woman, a mere 'pucellette' (l.393), a 'fillete de XVI ans' (l.273). Christine goes out of her way to stress that Joan is to be seen as an outstanding, representative member of the female sex, whose exploits surpass those of the most illustrious of Old Testament and Classical heroes, male and female, including Moses, Joshua, Gideon, Esther, Judith, Deborah, Hector and Achilles (see XXIII, XXV, XXVII, XXVIII, XXXVI). Such extraordinary prowess, she claims, has clearly brought honour and glory to all womankind: 'Hee! quel honneur au femenin/ Sexe! Que Dieu l'ayme il appert...' (ll.265–6). What makes this sequence of comparisons and contrasts particularly effective is the fact that it betrays the same kind of irony and gentle humour that Christine put to such good use in some of her earliest and most successful writings on the role and status of women (notably, the *Epistre au dieu d'Amours* of 1399). Apart from the ironical use which she makes of the diminutives 'pucellette' 'fillete' (ll.393, 273), one could point to the deliberate way in which she underlines the contrast between 'male' and 'female' in the following lines: 'Car, se Dieu fist par Josué/ Des miracles à si grant somme,/ Conquerant lieux, et jus rué/ Y furent maint, il estoit *homme*/ Fort et puissant. Mais, toute somme,/ *Une femme* – simple bergiere –/ Plus preux qu'onc *homs* ne fut à Romme!' (ll.193–9)...' Hee! quel honneur au *femenin/ Sexe*! Que Dieu l'ayme il appert,/ Quant tout ce grant pueple chenin,/ Par qui tout le regne ert desert,/ Par *femme* est sours et recouvert,/ Ce que C^{m} *hommes* /fait/ n'eussent,/ Et les traictres mis à desert' (ll.265–271)...' Donc desur tous les *preux* passez,/ *Ceste* doit porter la couronne,/ Car ses faiz ja monstrent assez/ Que plus prouesse Dieu lui donne/

Qu'à *tous ceulz* de qui l'on raisonne' (ll.345–49). Although the debate of the *Roman de la Rose* must have lost some of its fervour by 1429, one senses from these lines that Christine took great delight in being offered one last opportunity to score a point against old adversaries. For that reason, therefore, it is appropriate to see the *Ditié*, on one level, as the fitting conclusion to a whole sequence of works written by Christine in defence of the feminist cause.

At the conclusion of this brief survey of the different thematic elements that have gone into Christine's poem it remains to stress that while each has been defined and discussed separately for the sake of analysis, in the poem itself each has been fully integrated as part of a coherent whole. The different elements (religious, patriotic, feminist) are skilfully fused and blended together by a number of factors. Firstly, they are all contained within an overall structure which is itself cohesive and unified; secondly, they have all been woven round a single central figure, Joan of Arc; thirdly, Christine handles them simultaneously in such a way that each is made to highlight and reinforce the other; and finally, and perhaps most importantly of all, taken together they reflect a single, fundamental conception that underlies not just the *Ditié* but all of Christine's previous work, namely, the belief that women have a role of paramount importance to play in the unfolding of God's designs for the world in general and for France in particular. In the light of these considerations, therefore, it is clear that the *Ditié*, both from a structural and thematic point of view, reveals a greater degree of craftmanship and organising skill than has usually been allowed. That said and stressed, it remains true of course that a large part of the interest of the *Ditié* derives from the themes themselves (as distinct from Christine's handling of them). As this analysis has shown, the *Ditié* is at once a unique and representative work which, in capturing the sense of wonder and thankfulness that all of France must have felt at Joan's victories, also draws together some of Christine's central ideas and preoccupations; as such (and not just because it happens to be Christine's last surviving work) it fully merits Mathilde Laigle's apt description of it in her study of the *Livre des Trois Vertus*, as 'le testament littéraire de Christine de Pisan.'[22]

Style and Versification

The few comments which have been made to date on the style and versification of the *Ditié* have been almost wholly critical. Marie-Josèphe Pinet, one of Christine's most sympathetic biographers, finds the poem to be an 'assez pauvre chose, prise en soi',[23] while de Roche and Wissler in the introduction to their edition put forward the view that 'cette dernière effusion de son talent est loin d'être un chef d'oeuvre et n'a rien ajouté à la gloire littéraire de celle qui en son beau temps, malgré les "Mutacions de fortune", traitait avec sapience et maîtrise les grands thèmes d'amour et qui tournait naguère si gracieusement lais, virelais, rondeaux et ballades. Ces 61 strophes de huit vers octosyllabes frisent trop la prose pour être fameuses. Même en imputant une part de ses imperfections et défaillances à l'étourderie d'un copiste maladroit, l'on constate à regret que la plume du poète n'a plus la grâce fleurie ni la souple élégance d'autrefois; ces fins de strophe arrivent mal, la facture et le rythme de ses vers se sont faits rudes et malaisés'.[24] While one can question the general assumption which seems to underlie de Roche and Wissler's remarks (i.e. that one should look for and expect to find in the *Ditié* the same 'grâce fleurie' and the 'souple élégance' which characterised Christine's love poetry), it remains true that the poem does reveal many of the apparent weaknesses which they raise and some additional ones which they do not explicitly mention. The sentence-structure at times produces an abrupt, staccato-effect (see, for example, the numerous short rhetorical questions, exclamations and asides which punctuate the whole poem, giving it a distinctly emotional, 'oral' quality e.g. ll.87, 95, 104, 176, 360, 375, 376); more frequently, however, the syntax reflects Christine's prose style which, modelled as it was on the rhythms and tortuous complexity of the Latin period, tends to dislocate normal verse patterns (see, for example, ll.73–84, 97–110). The exact grammatical function of a word or group of words is not always immediately clear (see, for example, ll.119, 136, 215), with the result that on occasion an alternative punctuation would not only be possible but also perfectly acceptable (e.g. ll.306–7: 'Car jamais n'aurez beau gibier!/ En France ne menez voz sornes!' or 'Car jamais n'aurez beau gibier/ En France! Ne menez voz sornes!'). The sense of exhilaration which Christine experiences at Joan's coming at times finds expression in colourless, repetitive formulae which, taken by themselves, never seem to do full justice to the obvious sincerity and intensity of the emotion which underlies them (see, for example, l.54 'Car ce est digne de memoire', l.85 'Chose est bien digne de memoire', l.87 'chose est voire', and l.104 'chose est nouvelle'). Finally, a few slips in rhyme and versification confirm the view put forward earlier, on chronological grounds, that the poem was probably very hastily conceived and executed (e.g. *prime* and *fine* ll.37 and 39 are closer to assonance than rhyme; *huitain* LVIII shows what is obviously an accidental departure from the fixed rhyme pattern: *ababbcbc*— in l.463, the second last line of the stanza, the *a*–rhyme of 457 and 459 is repeated).

All of these points – which range over questions of syntax, grammar, rhythm and versification – clearly require one to concede that at the level of the line or the stanza the poem does not reveal the same degree of skill discernible in its overall structure, that Christine's 'manner', in other words, does not always match up the splendid subject-matter of her poem. Yet when due allowance has been made for the rough edges which the poem undoubtedly has, it is important to stress (and readers of mediaeval poetry who prefer Béroul to Thomas will confirm this) that rough edges and imperfections need not automatically be equated with overall artistic ineffectiveness: it still remains possible to argue, as we propose to do, for a more positive assessment of Christine's achievement. In doing this, we shall concentrate on what we believe to be the *Ditié*'s most striking characteristic, its dramatic energy and vitality which is in fact created by many of the poem's so-called 'imperfections', and sustained and reinforced by an additional factor which has not yet been mentioned, namely, the skill with which Christine sometimes exploits the expressive value of the *sound* of her verse.

The first of these points can be illustrated briefly by looking in closer detail at a number of representative *huitains* which include some of the specific faults mentioned, such as the tortuous syntax, abrupt rhythms and the dislocation of normal grammatical or verse patterns. In the opening twelve lines of the poem which form a single sentence linking *huitains* I and II and thus dispense with the expected full pause at the end of l.8, it is important to note that it is the syntactical complexity itself which most effectively captures Christine's sense of triumph and exultation. In these lines the main clause ('Ore à prime me prens à rire' l.8) is skilfully thrown into strong relief by being deliberately delayed through the sequence of subordinate clauses (ll.1–7) and by then being immediately repeated with variation and inversion ('A rire bonement de joie/Me prens...') in ll.9–10: 'Je, Christine, qui ay plouré/ XI ans en abbaye close,/ Où j'ay tousjours puis demouré/ Que Charles (c'est estrange chose!),/ Le filz du roy, se dire l'ose,/ S'en fouy de Paris de tire,/ Par la traïson là enclose,/ Ore à prime me prens à rire;// A rire bonement de joie/ Me prens...' *Huitains* X and XI are linked by an equally complex single sentence which nonetheless dynamically conveys Christine's sense of wonder at the workings of divine Providence: 'Qui vit doncques chose avenir/ Plus hors de toute opinion/ (Qui à noter et souvenir/ Fait bien en toute region),/ Que France (de qui mention/ On faisoit que jus ert ruée)/ Soit, par divine mission,/ Du mal en si grant bien muée,// Par tel miracle voirement/ Que, se la chose n'yert notoire/ Et evident quoy et comment,/ Il n'est homs qui le peüst croire?' In ll.203–6 and 449–54 it is the elliptical mid-sentence changes of grammatical construction which help to convey, in the first example, Christine's breathless excitement at Joan's achievement and, in the second, the urgency of her desire to see all France unite under Charles VII: 'Car tous les preux au long aler/ Qui ont esté, ne s'appareille/ Leur prouesse à ceste qui veille/ A bouter hors noz ennemis' ... 'Et vous, toutes villes rebelles,/ Et gens qui avez regnié/ Vostre seigneur, et ceulx et celles/ Qui pour autre l'avez nié,/ Or soit après aplanié/ Par doulceur, requerant pardon!' The fact that each successive line in *huitain* XLIII can be read almost as if it were a self-contained unit produces an abrupt staccato-effect: yet it is this very abruptness which dramatically underlines Christine's unshakeable faith in the future destiny of both Joan and Charles: 'Des Sarradins fera essart,/ En conquerant la Saintte Terre./ Là menra Charles, que Dieu gard!/ Ains qu'il muire, fera tel erre./ Cilz est cil qui la doit conquerre./ Là doit-elle finer sa vie,/ Et l'un et l'autre gloire acquerre./ Là sera la chose assovye.' In *huitains* XIII–XIV, particularly ll.101–10, it is the irregular rhythms produced by the way in which Christine breaks up the expected verse pattern which to a large extent convey her sense of wonder and restless excitement at Joan's miraculous exploits: 'Mais, Dieu grace, or voiz ton renon/Hault eslevé par la Pucelle,/ Qui a soubzmis soubz ton penon/ Tes ennemis (chose est nouvelle!)// En peu de temps; que l'on cuidoit/ Que ce feust com chose impossible/ Que ton pays, qui se perdoit,/ Reusses jamais. Or est visible–/ Ment tien, [puis que] qui que nuisible/ T'ait esté, tu l'as recouvré!' What clearly emerges, then, from these examples is that some of the features which have sometimes been dismissed as faults or weaknesses paradoxically work into the poem a robust dynamic quality appropriate to its central themes.

This impression of robustness is reinforced by the way in which Christine sometimes exploits the expressive value of the *sound* of her verse. Of the technical devices to which she has recourse by far the most common are alliteration and internal rhyme or assonance which are used with vigorous effect not only within a very large number of individual lines (e.g. 8, 24, 88, 150, 167–8, 223–4, 264, 296, 298, 352) but in whole *huitains* as well. Three particularly striking examples will suffice to illustrate this general point, the first being provided by *huitain* VI: 'Or faisons feste à nostre roy!/ Que tresbien soit-il revenu!/ Resjoïz de son noble arroy,/ Alons trestous, grant et menu,/ Au devant - nul ne soit tenu!–/ Menant joie le saluer,/ Louant Dieu, qui l'a maintenu,/ Criant "Noël" en hault huer.' Here a series of alliterations (in *f, n, r, tr*) and the insistent repetition of similar vowel-sounds at approximately the same point in six out of the eight lines, i.e. at the second or third syllable of ll.41, 44, 45, 46, 47, 48 (*faisons, alons, devant, menant, louant, criant*), make the appeal formulated in this *huitain* all the more urgent and emphatic. The second illustration is provided by *huitains* XXXV–VI, in particular ll.278–83: 'Et devant elle vont fuyant/ Les ennemis, ne nul n'y dure./ Elle fait ce, mains yeulx voiant,// Et d'eulx va France descombrant,/ En recouvrant chasteaulx et villes./ Jamais force ne fu si grant...' In these lines the deliberate repetition of similar nasal vowel-sounds both at the rhyme and internally (*devant, vont, fuyant, voiant, descombrant, recouvrant, grant*) produces an equally insistent effect, designed this time to highlight Christine's delight at the swiftness of Joan's victories. The third and last example which we have selected is represented by *huitain* XLIII: 'Des Sarradins fera essart,/ En conquerant la Saintte Terre./ Là menra Charles, que Dieu gard!/ Ains qu'il muire, fera tel erre./ Cilz est cil qui la doit conquerre./ Là doit-elle finer sa vie,/ Et l'un et l'autre gloire acquerre./ Là sera la chose assovye'. Here alliterative effects (*Sarradins, essart, Saintte, Cilz, cil, sera, chose, assovye*) and a dense pattern of sounds which take up and thereby highlight the–*a* of the future tenses *fera, menra, fera* in ll. 337, 339, 340 and 344 (*Sarradins, essart* l.337, *Sainte* l.339, *là* ll.339, 342, 344, *Charles, gard* l.339, *acquerre* l.343) give forceful expression to Christine's faith in the divinely-ordained, predetermined nature of Joan's life.

In the light of all these points, then, it is clear that, whatever reservations one may have about specific details in Christine's handling of her material, the *Ditié de Jehanne d'Arc* is a brisk, vigorous and compelling poem, and entitled as such to a more generous assessment than the one which it has hitherto usually been accorded. Though certainly lacking in the great imaginative and expressive power that a d'Aubigné or an Aragon could and did bring to war-poetry, it has nonetheless a number of positive literary qualities which raise it above the level of the mere 'chronique rimée' with which it has sometimes been too readily associated.[25] Robert Sabatier has perhaps best summed up both the strength and the limitations of Christine's achievement when he describes the *Ditié*, in *La Poésie du Moyen Age*, as 'la meilleure oeuvre écrite à son époque à propos d'un événement qui n'a jamais fait naître l'*Iliade* française attendue.'[26]

FOOTNOTES TO INTRODUCTION

1. For a general survey of literary works inspired by Joan of Arc, see Ingvald Raknem, *Joan of Arc in History, Legend and Literature,* Universitetsforlaget Oslo-Bergen-Tromsö, 1971. The *Ditié* is discussed on pp. 34–38.

2. S. Solente, *Christine de Pisan. Extrait de l'Histoire littéraire de la France,* tome XL, Paris, Imprimerie Nationale, 1969, p.74; 'Un traité inédit de Christine de Pisan: l'Epistre de la prison de vie humaine', *Bibliothèque de l'Ecole des Chartes,* 1924, t.85, p.268.

3. See pp.6 and 174 of the *Avision-Christine,* ed. Sister Mary Louis Towner, The Catholic University of America Studies in Romance Languages and Literatures, vol. VI, originally published Washington D.C., 1932 and reprinted 1969 by AMS Press, New York.

4. J. Gough Nichols' edition for the Roxburghe Club, London, 1860, p.54; see also pp.xxxiii–iv of George F. Warner's introduction to Stephen Scrope's translation *The Epistle of Othea to Hector,* London, Roxburghe Club, 1904; G. F. Warner and J. P. Gilson, *Catalogue of Western Manuscripts in the Old Royal and King's Collections,* British Museum, 4 vols., 1921.

5. In ll.10–11, 28–32 Christine refers to the departure of winter and the return of spring.

6. There are no clear grounds for assuming, as Anatole France does in his *Vie de Jeanne d'Arc,* Paris, Calmann–Lévy, ed. of 1924, vol.2, p.33, that *huitains* XLVIII–LXI were the only ones to have been written after the coronation of 17 July. *Huitain* V, for example, presents Charles as 'venant comme roy *coronné*'.

7. *Festschrift Louis Gauchat,* Aarau, 1926, p.332.

8. In the section on the English, XXXIX–XLV, Christine also evokes Joan's future achievements.

9. In quotations a single oblique stroke marks the end of a line, two oblique strokes the end of a *huitain.*

10. On this distinction between Fortune and Providence see also Part III of the *Avision–Christine,* ed.cit. particularly pp.169 *et seq.*

11. See Dorothy G. Wayman's article 'The Chancellor and Jeanne d'Arc February–July A.D. 1429', *Franciscan Studies,* XVII, 1957, pp.273–305; Régine Pernoud, *La Libération d'Orléans,* Paris, Gallimard, 1969, p.168, note 2.

12. *Christine de Pisan 1364–1430. Etude biographique et littéraire,* Paris, Champion, 1927, *Bibliothèque du XVe siècle,* 35, p.195.

13. Christine's intense patriotism is all the more remarkable when one recalls that she was herself, of course, of Italian birth.

14. Published in *Oeuvres poétiques de Christine de Pisan,* ed. M. Roy, Paris, Fimin Didot, 1886–96, 3 vols., *Société des Anciens Textes Français,* vol. 1, pp. 240–4.

15. *Livre du Chemin de Long Estude,* ed. Robert Püschel, Berlin, Damköhler, and Paris, Le Soudier, 1881 and 1887, ll.303–50, 2635–46; *Livre de la Mutacion de Fortune,* ed. S. Solente, Paris, Picard, 1959–66, 4 vols., *Société des Anciens Textes Français,* vol. 1, pp. 146–7; *Avision–Christine, ed. cit.,* Part 1, pp. 73–108.

16. Ed. Charity Cannon Willard, The Hague, Mouton, 1958, pp. 61, 91, 135 respectively.

17. *Livre du Chemin de Long Estude, ed.cit.,* ll.4995–5042 and 6255–9; *Livre du Corps de Policie,* ed. Robert H. Lucas, Genève, Droz, 1967, pp. 1–102; *Le Livre de la Paix, ed.cit.,* pp.124–6, 136–81.

18. It is clear once again that Christine's portrait of the ideal monarch is much influenced by her admiration for Charles V.

19. E.M.D. Robineau, *Christine de Pisan, sa vie et ses oeuvres,* Saint-Omer, Fleury–Lemaire, 1882, p.387, quoted by Marie–Josèphe Pinet, *op.cit.* p.427.

20. On feminism, see Helen Ruth Finkel, 'The Portrait of the Woman in the Works of Christine de Pisan', *Les Bonnes Feuilles,* vol.iii, no.ii, Fall 1974, pp.138–151, Pennsylvania State University; Lula McD. Richardson, *The Forerunners of Feminism in French Literarure of the Renaissance,* John Hopkins Studies in Romance Literatures and Languages vol.XII, Baltimore, 1929, pp.12–34; Rose Rigaud, *Les idées féministes de Christine de Pisan,* Thèse présentée à la Faculté des Lettres de l'Université de Neuchâtel, Slatkine Reprints, 1973; Jean Lamac, *Histoire de la littérature féminine en France,* 8e ed., 'Les documentaires', Editions KRA, Paris, n.d.

21. In, for example, the *Epistre au Dieu d'Amours* (1399), the *Dit de la Rose* (1402), *Livre de la Mutacion de Fortune* (1403), *ed.cit.,* vol.2, ll.5379–94, the *Cité des Dames* (1405) and *Le Livre des Trois Vertus* (1405). See also *Oeuvres poétiques ed.cit.* vol.1, 'Autres Balades' II, III, IV, XII, XXXVII, and the rondeau that precedes XXXVII; vol.3, p.39, number LXXVII of 'Les Enseignemens moraux', and Kenneth Varty ed. *Ballades, Rondeaux and Virelais,* Leicester University Press, 1965, pp.118–9, 162–3. On the debate on the *Roman de la Rose,* see Charles Frederick Ward, *The Epistles on the Romance of the Rose and other Documents in the Debate,* Chicago, 1911, and Peter Potansky, *Der Streit um den Rosenroman* (Münchener Romanistische Arbeiten XXXIII, Munich, Fink, 1972: Enid McLeod, *The Order of the Rose. The Life and Ideas of Christine de Pizan,* London, Chatto and Windus, 1976, pp.62–76.

22. *Livre des Trois Vertus,* Paris, Champion, 1912, *Bibliothèque du XVe siècle,* 16, p.371.

23. Marie–Josèphe Pinet, *op.cit.* p.195.

24. *Festschrift Louis Gauchat,* Aarau, 1925, p.333.

25. See titles of previous editions of the *Ditié*, and Marie–Josèphe Pinet *op.cit.* p.181 and p.416. Despite all their criticisms, de Roche and Wissler, it should be pointed out, consider the poem to be more than a rhymed chronicle. They rightly state in their introduction (p.333): 'Un souffle religieux les traverse (i.e. les strophes de Christine) et les empêche de tomber au niveau d'une simple chronique rimée.' We have tried to argue, of course, that there are positive literary qualities in the *Ditié* which would also justify this assertion.

26. Paris, A. Michel, 1975, p.327.

TABLE OF EVENTS: HISTORICAL BACKGROUND TO THE *DITIE DE JEHANNE D'ARC*

1418 Victory of the Burgundians over the Armagnacs. Entry of the Burgundians into Paris. The Dauphin Charles forced to flee to Bourges (and Christine to an 'abbaye close').

1419 Assassination of the Duke of Burgundy, Jean sans Peur, on the bridge at Montereau, 10 September. Philippe le Bon succeeds his father as Duke of Burgundy, and allies himself with Henry V of England.

1420 Treaty of Troyes. The Dauphin Charles disinherited, Henry V to marry Charles' sister Catherine and become King of France after death of Charles VI.

1422 Death of Henry V and Charles VI. The Dauphin assumes title of Charles VII.

1428 Joan of Arc at Vaucouleurs in May. Siege of Orléans begun by the English on 12 October.

1429 Joan at Chinon, 23 February or 6 March; interrogation at Poitiers, March-April; relief of Orléans, 8 May; coronation of Charles VII at Rheims, 17 July; Charles and Joan at Vailly on 22 July, at Soissons from 23 to 28 July, at Château-Thierry on 29 July.

Ditié de Jehanne d'Arc completed on 31 July.

TABLE OF CHRISTINE DE PISAN'S MAIN WORKS

VERSE

c. 1393–c. 1410	*Cent Ballades, Virelais, Ballades d'Estrange Façon, Lais, Rondeaux, Jeux à vendre, Autres Ballades, Encore Autres Ballades, Complaintes, Livre des Trois Jugements, Oroyson Nostre Dame, Les XV Joyes Nostre Dame, Oroyson de Nostre Seigneur, Enseignements moraux, Proverbes moraux, Cent Ballades d'Amant et de Dame.*
1399	*Epistre au Dieu d'Amours*
1400	*Dit de Poissy, Débat de deux amants*
1402	*Dit de la Rose*
1403	*Dit de la Pastoure, Livre du Chemin de Long Estude, Livre de la Mutacion de Fortune.*
1404	*Epistre à Eustache Morel*
1405	*Livre du Duc des Vrais Amants*
1429	*Ditié de Jehanne d'Arc*

PROSE

c. 1400	*Epistre d'Othéa à Hector*
1402	*Epistres sur le Roman de la Rose*
1404	*Livre des fais et bonnes meurs du sage roy Charles V*
1405	*Livre de la Cité de Dames* *Livre des Trois Vertus ou Trésor de la Cité des Dames* *Avision-Christine* *Lettre à Isabeau de Bavière*

1406	*Livre de Prudence* *Livre de la Prod'hommie de l'homme*
1407	*Livre du Corps de Policie*
1409	*Sept Psaumes allegorisés*
1410	*Livre des fais d'armes et de chevalerie* *Lamentacion sur les maux de la France*
1413	*Livre de la Paix*
1416–8	*Epistre de la Prison de vie humaine*
c. 1420	*Heures de contemplacion sur la Passion de Nostre Seigneur*

DITIÉ DE JEHANNE D'ARC: DESCRIPTION OF THE PLATES

Plate I	Berne ms. 205	f. 62^r *huitains* I–V
Plate II	Berne ms. 205	ff. 62^v *huitains* VI–VII and 63^r *huitains* VIII–XII
Plate III	Berne ms. 205	ff. 63^v *huitains* XIII–XVII and 64^r *huitains* XVIII–XXII
Plate IV	Berne ms. 205	ff. 64^v *huitains* XXIII–XXVII and 65^r *huitains* XXVIII–XXXII
Plate V	Berne ms. 205	ff. 65^v *huitains* XXXIII–XXXVII and 66^r *huitains* XXXVIII–XLII
Plate VI	Berne ms. 205	ff. 66^v *huitains* XLIII–XLVII and 67^r *huitains* XLVIII–LII
Plate VII	Berne ms. 205	ff. 67^v *huitains* LIII–LVII and 68^r *huitains* LVIII–LXI
Plate VIIIa	Grenoble ms. U 909 Rés	f. 101^r *huitains* XXXV, XLIV–XLVI (11. 1–3)
Plate VIIIb	Carpentras ms. 390	f. 88^v *huitains* XLVIII (11. 2–8) – LI (11. 1–3)

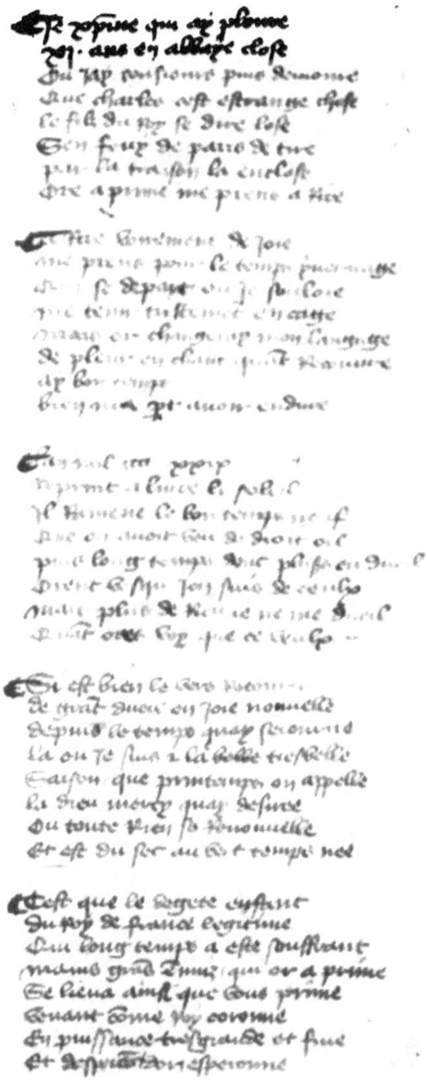

Plate I

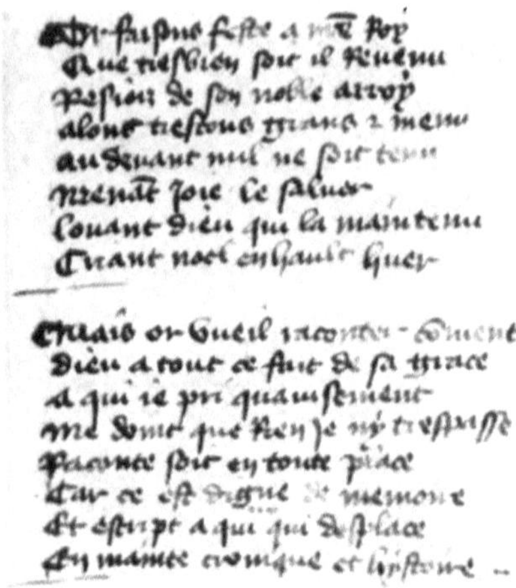
Or faisons feste a nostre roy
Que tres bien soit il revenu
Resjoiz de son noble arroy
Alons tres tous grans et menu
Au devant nul ne soit tenu
Menant joie le saluer
Louant dieu qui la maintenu
Criant noel en hault huer

Mais or vueil raconter comment
Dieu a tout ce fait de sa grace
A qui je pri quavisement
Me doint que rien je ny trespasse
Racompte soit en toute place
Car ce est digne de memoire
Et escript a qui qui desplace
En mainte cronique et histoire

Plate II

Oyez par tout l'univers monde
Chose sur toute merveillable
Notez se Dieu en qui habonde
Toute grace est point secourable
Au droit en fin c'est fait notable
Considere le present cas
Si soit aux decevans valable
Que fortune a flati a cas

Et note comment esbahie
Ne se doit nul pour infortune
Se voiant a grant tort hair
Et comment sur par voix commune
Voie amee tousjours n'est une
Fortune qui a nuit a maint
Car Dieu qui aux tors fait rencune
Relieve en qui espoir maint

Qui vit doncques chose avenir
Plus hors de toute opinion
Qui a noter et souvenir
Fait bien en toute region
Que France de qui mention
On faisoit que jus est ruee
Soit par divine mission
Du mal en si grant bien muee

Par tel miracle vrayement
Que se la chose n'ert notoire
Et evident quoy et comment
Il n'est homs qui le peust croire
Chose est bien digne de memoire
Que Dieu par une vierge tendre
Ait adès voulu chose est voire
Sur France si grant grace estendre

O quel honneur a la couronne
De France par divine preuve
Car par les graces qu'il lui donne
Il appert comment il l'appreuve
Et que plus foy qu'autre part treuve
En l'estat royal dont je lis
Que oncques ce n'est pas chose neuve
En foy n'errerent fleurs de lis./-

Et tu charles roy des francois
VII.e dicellui hault nom
Qui si grant guerre as eue ancois
Que bien ten prensist se peu non
Mais dieu grace or voiz ton renon
Hault esleve par la pucelle
Qui a soubzmis soubz ton penon
Tes ennemis chose est nouvelle

En peu de temps que lon cuidoit
Que ce feust ce chose impossible
Que ton pays qui se perdoit
Reusses jamais or est visible
ment tien quiconque nuisible
Tant este tu las recouvre
Cest par la pucelle sensible
Dieu mercy qui y a ouvre

Si croy fermement que tel grace
Ne te soit de dieu donnee
Se a toy en temps et espace
Il nestoit de lui ordonnee
Quelque grant chose solempnee
A terminer et mettre a chief
Et quil tait donne destinee
Destre de tres grans fais le chief

Car ung roy de france doit estre
Charles filz de charles nomme
Qui sur tous rois sera grant maistre
Prophecie lont surnomme
Le cerf volant et consomme
Sera par cellui conquereur
Maint fait dieu la a ce nomme
Et en fin doit estre empereur

Tout ce est le prouffit de tame
Je prie a dieu que cellui soies
Et quil te doint sans le grief dame
Tant vivre quencores tu voies
Tes enfans grans et toutes joyes
Par toy et eulx soient en france
Mais en servant dieu toutes voies
Ne guerre ny face oultrance

Et jay espoir que bon seras
Droiturier et amant justice
Et tous autres passeras
Mais que orgueil ton fait ne honnisse
A ton peuple doulz et propice
Et craingnant dieu qui ta esleu
Pour son servant si as premisse
En as mais que faces ton deu

Et comment pourras tu jamais
Dieu mercier a souffisance
Servir doubter en tous tes fais
Qui de si grant contrariance
Ta mis a paix et toute france
Relevee de tel ruyne
Quant sa tresgrant sainte prudence
Ta fait de si grant honneur digne

Tu en soyes loue hault dieu
A toy gracier tous tenus
Sommes que donne temps et lieu
As ou ces biens sont avenus
Jointes mains grans et menus
Graces te rendons dieu celeste
Par qui nous sommes parvenus
A paix et hors de grant tempeste

Et toy pucelle beneuree
Y dois tu estre obliee
Puis que dieu ta tant honnouree
Que as la corde desliee
Qui tenoit france estroit liee
Te pourroit on assez louer
Quant ceste terre humiliee
Par guerre as fait de paix douer

Tu Johanne de bonne heure nee
Benoist soit cil qui te crea
Pucelle de dieu ordonnee
En qui le saint esperit rea
Sa grant grace en qui ot et a
Toute largesse de hault don
Non requeste ne te vea
Qui te rendra assez guerredon

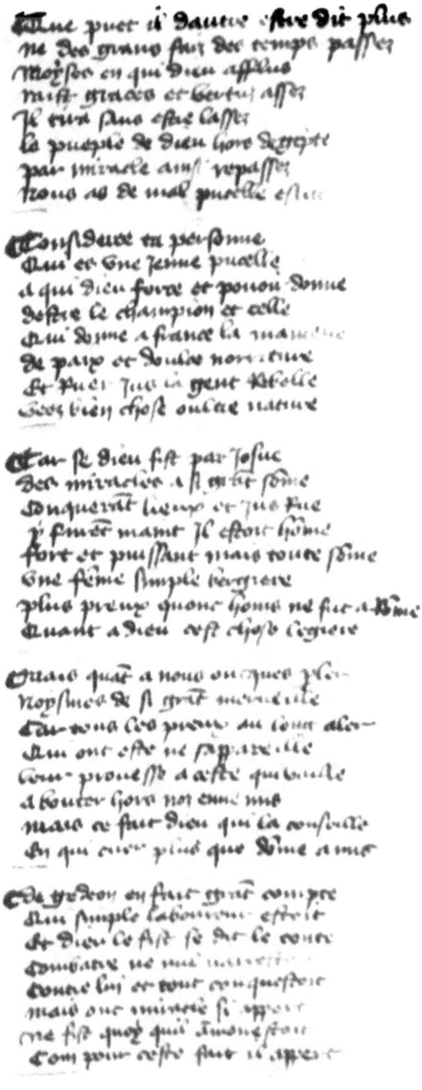

Que puet il dautre estre dit plus
Ne des grans faiz des temps passez
Moyses en qui dieu afflus
Mist graces et vertus assez
Il tira sans estre lassez
Le peuple de dieu hors degipte
Par miracle ainsi repassez
Nous as de mal pucelle eslite

Considere ta personne
Qui es une jeune pucelle
A qui dieu force et povoir donne
Destre le champion et celle
Qui donne a france la mamelle
De paix et doulce norriture
Et ruer jus la gent rebelle
Vees bien chose oultre nature

Car se dieu fist par josue
Des miracles a si grant somme
Conquerant lieux et jus rue
Y furent maint il estoit homme
Fort et puissant mais toute somme
Une femme simple bergiere
Plus preux quonc homme ne fut a romme
Quant a dieu cest chose legiere

Mais quant a nous oncques parler
Noysmes de si grant merveille
Car touz les preux au temps ale
Qui ont este ne sappareille
Leur prouesse a ceste qui veille
A bouter hors noz ennemis
Mais ce fait dieu qui la conseille
En qui cuer plus que domme a mis

De gedeon en fait grant compte
Qui simple laboureur estoit
Et dieu le fist ce dit le conte
Combatre ne nul narrestoit
Contre lui et tout conquestoit
Mais onc miracle si appert
Ne fist quoy quil amonestoit
Com pour ceste fait il appert

Plate IV

Hester Judith et Delbora
Qui furent dames de grant pris
Par lesquelles dieu restora
Son pueple qui fort estoit pris
Et dautres plusers ay appris
Qui furent preuses ny ot celle
Mais miracles en a porpris
Plus a fait par ceste pucelle

Par miracle fut envoiee
Et divine amonicion
De lange de dieu convoiee
Au roy pour sa provision
Son fait nest pas illusion
Car bien a este esprouvee
Par conseil en conclusion
A leffect la chose est prouvee

Et bien este examinee
Et ains que lon lait voulu croire
Devant clers et sages menee
Pour enserchier se chose voire
Disoit ainçois quil fust notoire
Que dieu leust vers le roy tramise
Mais on a trouve en histoire
Qua ce faire elle estoit commise

Car merlin et sebile et bede
Plus de V^c ans a la virent
En esperit et pour remede
En france en leurs escrips la mirent
Et leur prophecies en firent
Disans quel pourteroit baniere
Es guerres françoises et dirent
De son fait toute la maniere

Et sa belle vie par foy
Monstre quelle est de dieu en grace
Par quoy on adjouste plus foy
A son fait car quoy quelle face
Tousjours a dieu devant la face
Quelle appelle sert et deprie
En fait en dit ne va en place
Ou sa devocion detrie

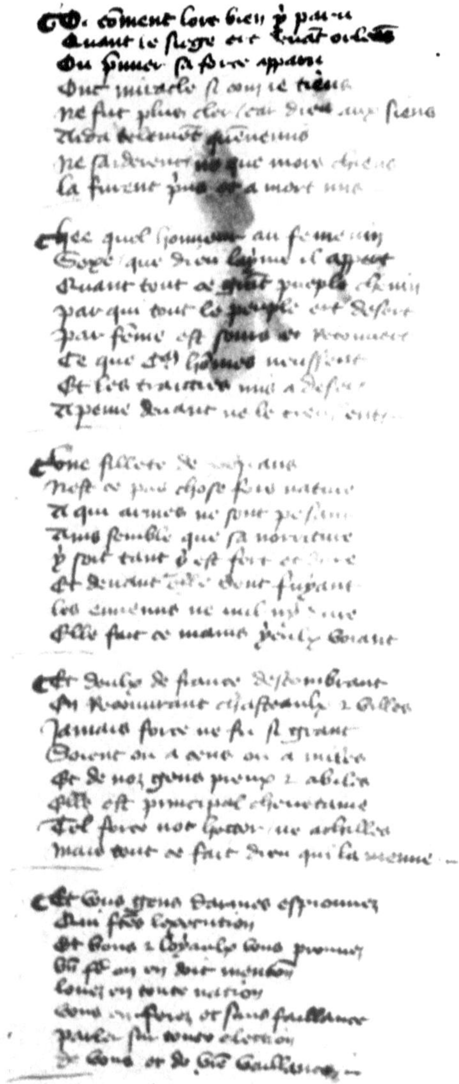
Oh. coment lors bien y paru
Quant le siege ert devant Orliens
Ou premier sa force apparut
Onc miracle si com je tiens
Ne fut plus cler car dieu aux siens
Aida telement que ennemis
Ne saiderent ne que mors chiens
La furent pris et a mort mis

Hee quel honneur au femenin
Sexe que dieu layme il appert
Quant tout ce grant peuple chenin
Par qui tout le peuple ert desert
Par feme est sours et recouvert
Ce que .v.m hommes neussent
Et les traictres mis a desert
A peine devant ne le creust on

Une fillete de xvi ans
Nest ce pas chose fors nature
A qui armes ne sont pesans
Ains semble que sa norriture
Y soit tant est fort et dure
Et devant elle vont fuyant
Les ennemis ne nul ny dure
Elle fait ce mains yeulx voiant

Et deulx va france descombrant
En recouvrant chasteaulx et villes
Jamais force ne fu si grant
Soient ou a cens ou a milles
Et de noz gens preux et abiles
Elle est principal chevetaine
Tel force not hector ne achilles
Mais tout ce fait dieu qui la menne

Et vous gens darmes esprouvez
Qui faictes lexecucion
Et bons et loyaulx vous prouvez
Bien fault quon en face mencion
Louez en toute nacion
Vous en serez et sans faillance
Parler sur toute elacion
De vous et de vo vaillance

Plate V

Qui ait sain corps et bien dispost
Pour le droit en peril s'endure
Et contre tous perilz ost
Vous, alez mettre a l'aventure.
Soiez constans, car je vous jure
Qu'en avrez gloire ou ciel et los,
Car qui se combat pour droiture
Paradis gaigne, dire l'os.

Or rebaissez, Anglois, voz cornes,
Car jamais n'aurez beau gibier.
En France ne menez voz sornes,
Matez estes en l'eschequier.
Vous ne pensiez pas l'autrier,
Où tant vous monstriez perilleux;
Mais n'estiez encor ou sentier
Où Dieu abat les orgueilleux.

Ja cuidiez France avoir gaignée
Et qu'elle vous deust demourer.
Autrement va, faulse mesgnée!
Vous irez ailleurs tabourer,
Se vous ne voulez assavourer
La mort, comme voz compaignons,
Que loups pourroient bien devourer,
Car mors gisent par les sillons.

Et sachez que par elle Anglois
Seront mis jus sans relever,
Car Dieu le veult, qui ot les vois
Des bons qu'ilz ont voulu grever!
Le sanc des occis sans lever
Crie contre eulx. Dieu ne veult plus
Le souffrir, ains les reprouver
Comme mauvais, il est conclus.

En chrestienté et l'Eglise
Sera par elle mis concorde.
Les mescreans dont on devise,
Et les herites de vie orde
Destruira, car ainsi l'acorde
Prophecie, qui l'a predit,
Ne point n'aura misericorde
De lieu qui la foy Dieu laidit.

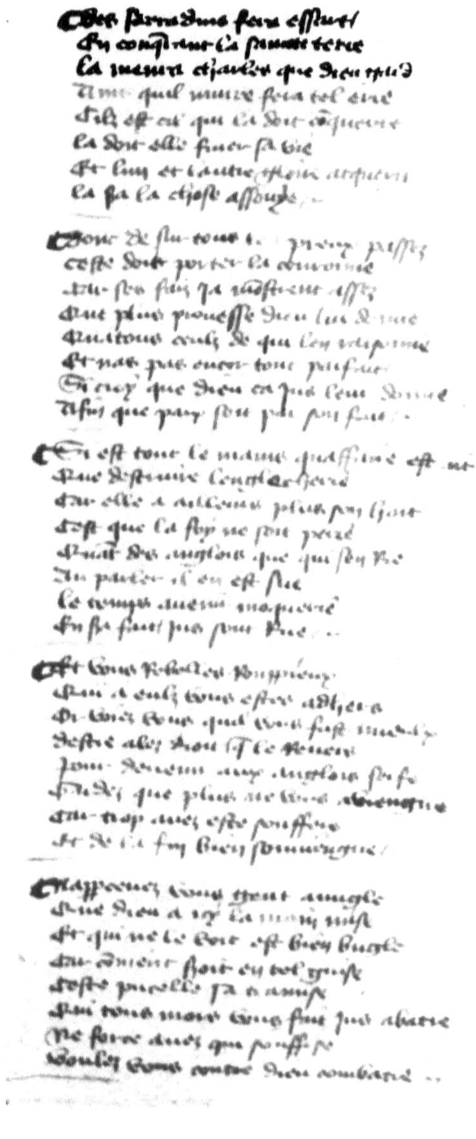

Plate VI

Par elle le roy mené au sacre
Que tousjours tenoit par la main
Plus grant chose oncques devant Acre
Ne fu faicte, car, pour certain,
Des contrediz y ot tout plain
Mais maulgré tous a grant noblesse
Y fu receu et tout a plain
Sacré et la ouy la messe.

En tres grant triumphe et puissance
Fu Charles couronné a Rains
L'an mil cccc sans doubtance
Du mois de juillet sauf et sains
Droit ou xviie jour
Du gens d'armes et barons mains
Et la fu v jours a sejour.

Avecques lui la pucelle
En retournant par son païs
Cité, chastel ne villete
Ne remaint amez ou haïs
Qu'il soit ou soient esbaïs
Ou asseurez les habitans
Se rendent. Pou sont envaïs
Tant sont sa puissance doubtans.

Voir est que aucuns de leur folie
Cuident resister, mais pou vault,
Car au derrain qui que s'en lie
A Dieu comparer le deffault.
C'est pour neant rendre leur fault
Vueillent ou non, n'y a si forte
Resistance qui a l'assault
De la pucelle ne soit morte.

Si qu'on ait fait grant assemblee
Cuidant son retour contredire
Et lui courir sus par emblee,
Mais plus n'y fault confort de mire
Car tous mors et pris tire a tire
Y ont esté les contrediz
Et envoyez com j'oy dire
En enfer ou en paradis.

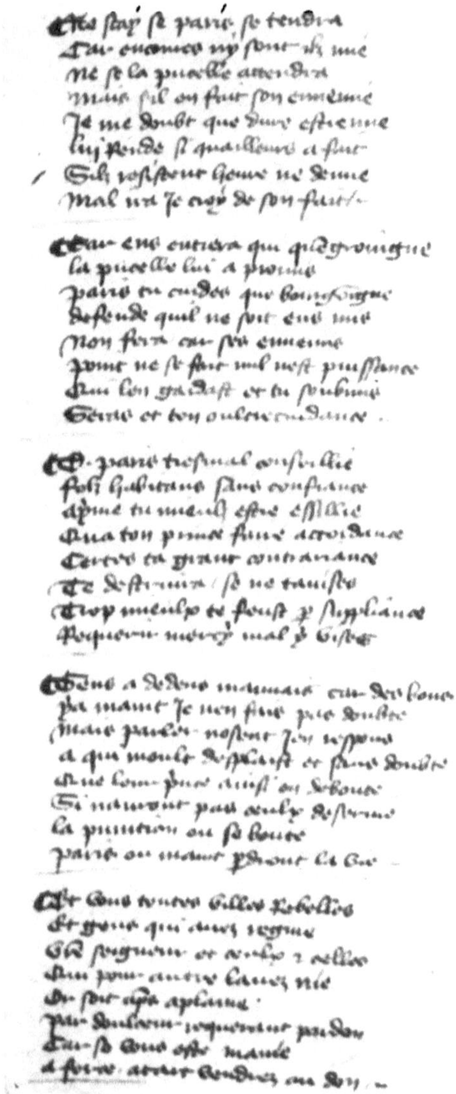

Plate VII

Et qui ne scet occasion
Plus vueille tenir quil prier
Ne fut chas dune maison
Car de sang espandre se deult
Mais au fort qui rendre ne veult
Par bel et doulceur ce qui est sien
Se par force en effusion
De sang le recouvre il fait bien

Helas il est si debonnaire
Qua chascun il veult pardonner
Et la pucelle lui fait faire
Qui ensuit dieu or ordonner
Vueillez voz cuers et vous donner
Comme loyaulx francois a lui
Et quant on lorra sermonner
Non serez repris de nullui

Si pry dieu quil mette en courage
A vous tous quainsi le faciez
Afin que le cruel orage
De ces guerres soit effaciez
Et que vostre vie passiez
En paix soubz vostre chief greignour
Si que jamais ne loffensiez
Et que vers vous soit bon seigneur

Amen

Donne ce ditie par xpine
Lan dessusdit mil .iiii^c.
Et xxix. le jour ou fine
Le mois de juillet mais jentens
Que aucuns se tendront mal contens
De ce quil contient car qui chiere
A embrunchie et les yeux pesans
Ne puet regarder la lumiere

Explicit ung tresbel ditie
fait par xpine

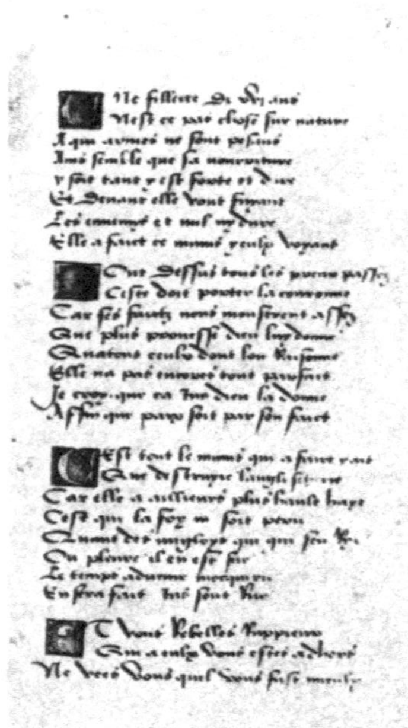

Plate VIIIa

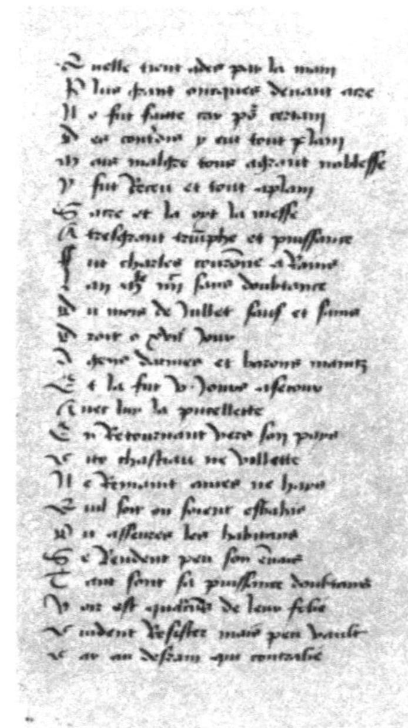

Plate VIIIb

DITIÉ DE JEHANNE D'ARC

I Je, Christine, qui ay plouré
Xl ans en abbaye close,
Où j'ay tousjours puis demouré
Que Charles (c'est estrange chose!),
Le filz du roy, se dire l'ose,
S'en fouÿ de Paris de tire,
Par la traïson là enclose,
Ore à prime me prens à rire;

II A rire bonement de joie
Me prens pour le temps yvernage
Qui se depart, où je souloie
Me tenir tristement en cage.
Mais or changeray mon langage
De pleur en chant, quant recouvré
Ay bon temps . . .
Bien ma part avoir enduré.

III L'an mil CCCCXXIX
Reprint à luire li soleil.
Il ramene le bon temps neuf
Qu'on [n'] avoit veü de droit oil
Puis long temps, dont plusers en dueil
Orent vesqu; j'en suis de ceulx.
Mais plus de rien je ne me dueil,
Quant ores voy ce que [je] veulx.

IV Si est bien le vers retourné
De grant dueil en joie nouvelle
Depuis le temps qu'ay sejourné
Là où je suis, et la tresbelle
Saison, que printemps on appelle,
La Dieu mercy, qu'ay desirée,
Où toute rien se renouvelle,
S'est du sec au vert temps tirée.

V C'est que le degeté enfant
Du roy de France legitime,
Qui long temps a esté souffrant
Mains grans ennuiz, qui or aprime,
Se lieva ainsi que vers prime,

Venant comme roy coronné
En puissance tresgrande et fine,
Et d'esperons d'or espronné.

VI Or faisons feste à nostre roy!
Que tresbien soit-il revenu!
Resjoïz de son noble arroy,
Alons trestous, grant et menu,
Au devant –– nul ne soit tenu! ––
Menant joie le saluer,
Louant Dieu, qui l'a maintenu,
Criant "Noël!" en hault huer.

VII Mais or vueil raconter comment
Dieu a tout ce fait de sa grace,
A qui je pri qu'avisement
Me doint, que rien je n'y trespasse.
Raconté soit en toute place,
Car ce est digne de memoire,
Et escript, à qui que desplace,
En mainte cronique et hystoire!

VIII Oyez par tout l'univers monde
Chose sur toute merveillable!
Notez se Dieu, en qui habonde
Toute grace, est point secourable
Au droit en fin. C'est fait notable,
Consideré le present cas!
Si soit aux deceüz valable,
Que Fortune a flati à cas!

IX Et note[z] comment esbahir
Ne se doit nul pour infortune,
Se voiant à grant tort haïr,
Et courir sus par voix commune!
Voie[z] comment tousjours n'est une
Fortune, qui a nuit à maint!
Car Dieu, qui aux tors faiz repune,
Ceulx relieve en qui espoir maint.

X Qui vit doncques chose avenir
Plus hors de toute opinion
(Qui à noter et souvenir
Fait bien en toute region),
Que France (de qui mention

On faisoit que jus ert ruée)
Soit, par divine mission,
Du mal en si grant bien muée,

XI Par tel miracle voirement
Que, se la chose n'yert notoire
Et evident quoy et comment,
Il n'est homs qui le peüst croire?
Chose est bien digne de memoire
Que Dieu, par une vierge tendre,
Ait adès voulu (chose est voire!)
Sur France si grant grace estendre.

XII O quel honneur à la couronne
De France par divine preuve!
Car par les graces qu'Il lui donne
Il appert comment Il l'apreuve,
Et que plus foy qu'autre part treuve
En l'estat royal, dont je lix
Qu'oncques (ce n'est pas chose neuve!)
En foy n'errerent fleurs de lix.

XIII Et tu, Charles, roy des François,
VIIe d'icellui hault nom,
Qui si grant guerre as eue ainçois
Que bien t'en prensist se peu non:
Mais, Dieu grace, or voiz ton renon
Hault eslevé par la Pucelle,
Qui a soubzmis soubz ton penon
Tes ennemis (chose est nouvelle!)

XIV En peu de temps; que l'on cuidoit
Que ce feust com chose impossible
Que ton pays, qui se perdoit,
Reusses jamais. Or est visible–
Ment tien, [puis que] qui que nuisible
T'ait esté, tu l'as recouvré!
C'est par la Pucelle sensible,
Dieu mercy, qui y a ouvré!

XV Si croy fermement que tel grace
Ne te seroit de Dieu donnée,
Se à toy, en temps et espace,
Il n'estoit de Lui ordonnée
Quelque grant chose solempnée

A terminer et mettre à chief,
Et qu'Il t'ait donné destinée
D'estre de tresgrans faiz le chief.

XVI Car ung roy de France doit estre
Charles, filz de Charles, nommé,
Qui sur tous rois sera grant maistre.
Propheciez l'ont surnommé
"Le Cerf Volant," et consomé
Sera par cellui conquereur
Maint fait (Dieu l'a à ce somé),
Et en fin doit estre empereur.

XVII Tout ce est le prouffit de t'ame.
Je prie à Dieu que cellui soies,
Et qu'Il te doint, sans le gref d'ame,
Tant vivre qu'encoures tu voyes
Tes enfans grans, et toutes joyes
Par toy et eulz soient en France!
Mais en servant Dieu toutesvoies,
Ne guerre [plus] n'y face oultrance!

XVIII Et j'ay espoir que bon seras,
Droiturier et amant justice,
Et [tres] tous autres passeras,
Mais qu'orgueil ton fait ne honnisse;
A ton pueple doulz et propice,
Et craingnant Dieu, qui t'a esleu
Pour son servant (si com premisse
En as), mais que faces ton deu.

XIX Et comment pourras-tu jamais
Dieu mercier à souffisance,
Servir, doubter en tous tes fais,
Qui de si grant contrariance
T'a mis à paix, et toute France
Relevée de tel ruyne,
Quant sa tressainte providence
T'a fait de si grant honneur digne?

XX Tu en soyes loué, hault Dieu!
A Toy gracier tous tenuz
Sommes, qui donné temps et lieu
As, où ces biens sont avenus.
[A] jointes mains, grans et menus,

Graces Te rendons, Dieu celeste,
Par qui nous sommes parvenus
A paix, et hors de grant tempeste!

XXI Et toy, Pucelle beneurée,
Y dois-tu estre obliée,
Puis que Dieu t'a tant honnorée
Que as la corde desliée
Qui tenoit France estroit liée?
Te pourroit-on assez louer
Quant ceste terre, humiliée
Par guerre, as fait de paix douer?

XXII Tu, Jehanne, de bonne heure née,
Benoist soit cil qui te créa!
Pucelle de Dieu ordonnée,
En qui le Saint Esprit réa
Sa grant grace, en qui ot et a
Toute largesse de hault don,
N'onc requeste ne te véa.
Qui te rendra assez guerdon?

XXIII Que puet-il d'autre estre dit plus
Ne des grans faiz des temps passez?
Moÿses, en qui Dieu afflus
Mist graces et vertuz assez,
Il tira, sans estre lassez,
Le pueple de Dieu hors d'Egipte
Par miracle. Ainsi repassez
Nous as de mal, Pucelle eslite!

XXIV Considerée ta personne,
Qui es une jeune pucelle,
A qui Dieu force et povoir donne
D'estre le champion et celle
Qui donne à France la mamelle
De paix et doulce norriture,
Et ruer jus la gent rebelle,
Véez bien chose oultre nature!

XXV Car, se Dieu fist par Josué
Des miracles à si grant somme,
Conquerant lieux, et jus rué
Y furent maint, il estoit homme
Fort et puissant. Mais, toute somme,

Une femme —— simple bergiere ——
Plus preux qu'onc homs ne fut à Romme!
Quant à Dieu, c'est chose legiere.

XXVI Mais quant à nous, oncques parler
N'oÿsmes de si grant merveille,
Car tous les preux au long aler
Qui ont esté, ne s'appareille
Leur prouesse à ceste qui veille
A bouter hors noz ennemis.
Mais ce fait Dieu, qui la conseille,
En qui cuer plus que d'omme a mis.

XXVII De Gedeon on fait grant compte,
Qui simple laboureur estoit,
Et Dieu le fist, ce dit le conte,
Combatre, ne nul n'arrestoit
Contre lui, et tout conquestoit.
Mais onc miracle si appert
Ne fist, quoy qu'Il ammonestoit,
Com pour ceste fait, il appert.

XXVIII Hester, Judith et Delbora,
Qui furent dames de grant pris,
Par lesqueles Dieu restora
Son pueple, qui fort estoit pris,
Et d'autres plusers ay apris
Qui furent preuses, n'y ot celle,
Mains miracles en a pourpris.
Plus a fait par ceste Pucelle.

XXIX Par miracle fut envoiée
Et divine amonition,
De l'ange de Dieu convoiée
Au roy, pour sa provision.
Son fait n'est pas illusion,
Car bien a esté esprouvée
Par conseil (en conclusion,
A l'effect la chose est prouvée),

XXX Et bien esté examinée
A, ains que l'on l'ait voulu croire,
Devant clers et sages menée
Pour enserchér se chose voire
Disoit, ainçois qu'il fust notoire

Que Dieu l'eust vers le roy tramise.
Mais on a trouvé en histoire
Qu'à ce faire elle estoit commise;

XXXI Car Merlin et Sebile et Bede,
Plus de V^{c} ans a la virent
En esperit, et pour remede
En France en leurs escripz la mirent,
Et leur[s] prophecies en firent,
Disans qu'el pourteroit baniere
Es guerres françoises, et dirent
De son fait toute la maniere.

XXXII Et sa belle vie, par foy,
Monstre qu'elle est de Dieu en grace;
Par quoy on adjouste plus foy
A son fait. Car, quoy qu'elle face,
Tousjours a Dieu devant la face,
Qu'elle appelle, sert et deprie
En fait, en dit; ne va en place
Où sa devotion detrie.

XXXIII O! comment lors bien y paru
Quant le siege ert devant Orliens,
Où premier sa force apparu!
Onc miracle, si com je tiens,
Ne fut plus cler, car Dieu aux siens
Aida telement, qu'ennemis
Ne s'aiderent ne que mors chiens.
Là furent prins et à mort mis.

XXXIV Hee! quel honneur au femenin
Sexe! Que Dieu l'ayme il appert,
Quant tout ce grant pueple chenin,
Par qui tout le regne ert desert,
Par femme est sours et recouvert,
Ce que C^{m} hommes [fait] n'eussent,
Et les traictres mis à desert!
A peine devant ne le creussent.

XXXV Une fillete de XVI ans
(N'est-ce pas chose fors nature?),
A qui armes ne sont pesans,
Ains semble que sa norriture
Y soit, tant y est fort et dure!

Et devant elle vont fuyant
Les ennemis, ne nul n'y dure.
Elle fait ce, mains yeulx voiant,

XXXVI Et d'eulx va France descombrant,
En recouvrant chasteaulx et villes.
Jamais force ne fu si grant,
Soient ou à cens ou à miles!
Et de noz gens preux et abiles
Elle est principal chevetaine.
Tel force n'ot Hector n'Achilles!
Mais tout ce fait Dieu, qui la menne.

XXXVII Et vous, gens d'armes esprouvez,
Qui faites l'execution,
Et bons et loyaulx vous prouvez,
Bien faire on en doit mention
(Louez en toute nation
Vous en serez!), et sans faillance
Parler sur toute election
De vous, et de vostre vaillance,

XXXVIII Qui sanc, corps et vie exposez
Pour le droit, en peine si dure,
Et contre tous perilz osez
Vous aler mettre à l'avanture.
Soiés constans, car je vous jure
Qu'en aurés gloire ou ciel et los!
Car qui se combat pour droiture
Paradis gaingne, dire l'os.

XXXIX Si rabaissez, Anglois, voz cornes
Car jamais n'aurez beau gibier!
En France ne menez voz sornes!
Matez estes en l'eschiquier.
Vous ne [le] pensiez pas l'autrier,
Où tant vous monstriez perilleux;
Mais n'estiez encour ou santier,
Où Dieu abat les orguilleux.

XL Ja cuidiés France avoir gaingnée,
Et qu'elle vous deust demourer.
Autrement va, faulse mesgnié[e]!
Vous irés ailleurs tabourer,
Se ne voulez assavourer

La mort, comme voz compaignons,
Que loups pevent bien devourer,
Car mors gisent par les sillons!

XLI
Et sachez que par elle Anglois
Seront mis jus sans relever,
Car Dieu le veult, qui oit les voiz
Des bons qu'ilz ont voulu grever!
Le sanc des occis sans lever
Crie contre eulz. Dieu ne veult plus
Le souffrir, ains les reprouver
Comme mauvais, il est conclus.

XLII
En Christianté et l'Eglise
Sera par elle mis concorde.
Les mescreans dont on devise,
Et les herites de vie orde
Destruira, car ainsi l'acorde
Prophecie, qui l'a predit,
Ne point n'aura misericorde
De lieu, qui la foy Dieu laidit.

XLIII
Des Sarradins fera essart,
En conquerant la Saintte Terre.
Là menra Charles, que Dieu gard!
Ains qu'il muire, fera tel erre.
Cilz est cil qui la doit conquerre.
Là doit-elle finer sa vie,
Et l'un et l'autre gloire acquerre.
Là sera la chose assovye.

XLIV
Donc desur tous les preux passez,
Ceste doit porter la couronne,
Car ses faiz ja monstrent assez
Que plus prouesse Dieu lui donne
Qu'à tous ceulz de qui l'on raisonne.
Et n'a pas encor tout parfait!
Si croy que Dieu ça jus l'adonne,
Afin que paix soit par son fait.

XLV
Si est tout le mains qu'à faire ait
Que destruire l'Englecherie,
Car elle a ailleurs plus son hait:
C'est que la Foy ne soit perie.
Quant des Anglois, qui que s'en rie

Ou pleure, il en est sué.
Le temps avenir moquerie
En sera fait. Jus sont rué!

XLVI Et vous, rebelles rouppieux,
Qui à eulz vous estes adhers,
Or voiez-vous qu'il vous fust mieulx
D'estre alez droit que le revers,
Pour devenir aux Anglois serfs.
Gardez que plus ne vous aviengne
(Car trop avez esté souffers),
Et de la fin bien [vous] souviengne!

XLVII N'appercevez-vous, gent avugle,
Que Dieu a icy la main mise?
Et qui ne le voit est bien bugle,
Car comment seroit en tel guise
Ceste Pucelle ça tramise
Qui tous mors vous fait jus abatre?
—— Ne force [n']avez qui souffise!
Voulez-vous contre Dieu combatre?

XLVIII N'a el le roy mené au sacre,
Que tousjours tenoit par la main?
Plus grant chose oncques devant Acre
Ne fu faite; car pour certain
Des contrediz y ot tout plain.
Mais, maulgré tous, à grant noblesse
Y fu receu, et tout à plain
Sacré, et là ouÿ la messe.

XLIX A tresgrant triumphe et puissance
Fu Charles couronné à Rains,
L'an mil CCCC, sans doubtance,
[Et XXIX, tout] sauf et sains,
Ou gens d'armes et barons mains,
Droit ou XVIIe jour
De juillet. [Pou plus ou pou mains,]
Par là fu V jours à sejour,

L Avecques lui la Pucellette.
En retournant par son païs,
Cité ne chastel ne villete
Ne remaint. Amez ou haÿs
Qu'il soit, ou soient esbaïs

Ou asseurez, les habitans
Se rendent. Pou sont envahis,
Tant sont sa puissance doubtans!

LI

Voir est qu'aucuns de leur folie
Cuident resister, mais peu vault,
Car au derrain, qui contralie,
A Dieu compere le deffault.
C'est pour neant. Rendre leur fault,
Vueillent ou non. N'y a si forte
Resistance qui à l'assault
De la Pucelle ne soit morte,

LII

Quoy qu'on ait fait grant assemblée,
Cuidant son retour contredire
Et lui courir sur par emblée;
Mais plus n'y fault confort de mire,
Car tous mors et pris tire à tire
Y ont esté les contrediz,
Et envoyez, com j'oÿ dire,
En Enfer ou en Paradis.

LIII

Ne sçay se Paris se tendra
(Car encoures n'y sont-ilz mie),
Ne se la Pucelle attendra,
Mais s'il en fait son ennemie,
Je me doubt que dure escremie
Lui rende, si qu'ailleurs a fait.
S'ilz resistent heure ne demie,
Mal ira, je croy, de son fait,

LIV

Car ens entrera, qui qu'en groingne!
— La Pucelle lui a promis.
Paris, tu cuides que Bourgoingne
Defende qu'il ne soit ens mis?
Non fera, car ses ennemis
Point ne se fait. Nul n'a puissance
Qui l'en gardast, et tu soubmis
Seras, et ton oultrecuidance!

LV

O Paris tresmal conseillié!
Folz habitans sans confiance!
Ayme[s]-tu mieulz estre essillié
Qu'à ton prince faire accordance?
Certes, ta grant contrariance

Te destruira, se ne t'avises!
Trop mieulx te feust par suppliance
Requerir mercy. Mal y vises!

LVI J'entens des mauvais, car des bons
Y a maint, je n'en fais pas doubte,
Mais parler n'osent, j'en respons,
A qui moult il desplaist sans doubte
Que leur prince ainsi on deboute.
Si n'auront pas ceulx deservie
La punition où se boute
Paris, où maint perdront la vie.

LVII Et vous, toutes villes rebelles,
Et gens qui avez regnié
Vostre seigneur, et ceulx et celles
Qui pour autre l'avez nié,
Or soit après aplanié
Par doulceur, requerant pardon!
Car se vous este[s] manié
A force, à tart vendrez au don.

LVIII Et qu'i[l] ne soit occision
Faite, retarde tant qu'il puet,
Ne sur char d'omme incision,
Car de sang espandre se deult.
Mais, au fort, qui rendre ne veult
Par bel et doulceur ce qu'est sien,
Se par force en effusion
De sang le recouvre, il fait bien.

LIX Helas! Il est si debonnaire
Qu'à chascun il veult pardonner!
Et la Pucelle lui fait faire,
Qui ensuit Dieu. Or ordonner
Vueillez voz cueurs et vous donner
Comme loyaulx François à lui!
Et quant on l'orra sermonner
N'en serés reprins de nulluy.

LX Si pry Dieu qu'Il mecte en courage
A vous tous qu'ainsy le faciez,
Afin que le cruel orage
De ces guerres soit effaciez,
Et que vostre vie passiez

En paix, soubz vostre chief greigneur,
Si que jamais ne l'offensiez
Et que vers vous soit bon seigneur.
Amen

LXI

Donné ce Ditié par Christine,
L'an dessusdit mil CCCC
Et XXIX, le jour où fine
Le mois de juillet. Mais j'entens
Qu'aucuns se tendront mal contens
De ce qu'il contient, car qui chiere
A embrunche, et les yeux pesans,
Ne puet regarder la lumiere.

Explicit ung tresbel Ditié fait par Christine.

A TRANSLATION OF THE DITIÉ DE JEHANNE D'ARC

I I, Christine, who have wept for eleven years in a walled abbey where I have lived ever since Charles (how strange this is!) the King's son—dare I say it?—fled in haste from Paris, I who have lived enclosed there on account of the treachery, now, for the first time, begin to laugh;

II I begin to laugh heartily for joy at the departure of the wintry season, during which I was wont to live confined to a dreary cage. But now I shall change my language from one of tears to one of song, because I have found the good season once again . . . well endured my share.

III In 1429 the sun began to shine again. It brings back the good, new season which had not really been seen for a long time—and because of that many people had lived out their lives in sorrow; I myself am one of them. But I no longer grieve over anything, now that I can see what I desire.

IV But since the time when I came to stay where I am the situation has completely changed, great sorrow has given way to new joy and, thanks be to God, the lovely season called Spring, which I have longed for and in which every creature/thing is renewed, has brought greenness out of barren winter.

V The reason is that the rejected child of the rightful King of France, who has long suffered many a great misfortune and who now approaches, rose up as if towards prime, coming as a crowned King in might and majesty, wearing spurs of gold.

VI Now let us greet out King! Welcome to him on his return! Overjoyed at the sight of his noble array, let us all, both great and small, step forward to greet him joyously – and let no one hold back – praising God, who has kept him safe, and shouting 'Noël!' in a loud voice.

VII But now I wish to relate how God, to whom I pray for guidance lest I omit anything, accomplished all this through His grace. May it be told everywhere, for it is worthy of being remembered, and may it be written down – no matter whom it may displease – in many a chronicle and history-book!

VIII Now hear, throughout the whole world, of something which is more wonderful than anything else! See if God, in whom all grace abounds, does not in the end support what is right. This is a fact worthy of note, given the matter in hand! And let it be of profit to the disillusioned, whom Fortune has cast down!

IX And note how, when someone finds himself quite unjustly attacked and hated on all sides, there is no need for such a person to feel dismayed by misfortune. See how Fortune, who has harmed many a one, is so inconstant, for God, who opposes all wrong deeds, raises up those in whom hope dwells.

X Did anyone, then, see anything quite so extraordinary come to pass (something that is well worth noting and remembering in every region), namely, that France (about whom it was said she had been cast down) should see her fortunes change, by divine command, from evil to such great good,

XI as the result, indeed, of such a miracle that, if the matter were not so well-known and crystal-clear in every aspect, nobody would ever believe it? It is a fact well worth remembering that God should nevertheless have wished (and this is the truth!) to bestow such great blessings on France, through a young virgin.

XII And what honour for the French crown, this proof of divine intervention! For all the blessings which God bestows upon it demonstrate how much He favours it and that He finds more faith in the Royal House than anywhere else; as far as it is concerned, I read (and there is nothing new in this) that the Lilies of France never erred in matters of faith.

XIII And you Charles, King of France, seventh of that noble name, who have been involved in such a great war before things turned out at all well for you, now, thanks be to God, see your honour exalted by the Maid who has laid low your enemies beneath your standard (and this *is* new!)

XIV in a short time; for it was believed quite impossible that you should ever recover your country which you were on the point of losing. Now it is manifestly yours for, no matter who may have done you harm, you have recovered it! And all this has been brought about by the intelligence of the Maid who, God be thanked, has played her part in this matter!

XV And I firmly believe that God would never have bestowed such grace upon you if it were not ordained by Him that you should, in the course of time, accomplish and bring to completion some great and solemn task; I believe too that He has destined you to be the author of very great deeds.

XVI For there will be a King of France called Charles, son of Charles, who will be supreme ruler over all Kings. Prophecies have given him the name of 'The Flying Stag', and many a deed will be accomplished by this conqueror (God has called him to this task) and in the end he will be emperor.

XVII All this is to the profit of your soul. I pray to God that you may be the person I have described, and that He grant you long life, to nobody's harm, so that you may yet see your children grown up; I pray too that all joy come to France because of you and them! But, as you serve God always, may war never cause havoc there again (*or* by emending *face* to *face[s]*: 'May you never wage war to the death there again!')

XVIII I hope that you will be good and upright, and a lover of justice and that you will surpass all others, provided your deeds are not tarnished by pride, that you will be gentle and well-disposed towards your people, that you will always love God who elected you as His servant (and you have a first manifestation of this), on condition that you do your duty.

XIX And how will you ever be able to thank God enough, serve and fear Him in all your deeds (for He has led you from such great adversity to peace and raised up the whole of France from such ruin) when His most holy providence made you worthy of such signal honour?

XX May You be praised for this, great God! It is our bounden duty to thank You who decreed time and place for these blessings to come about. With hands clasped, both great and small, we all thank You, Heavenly Lord, who have guided us through the great tempest into peace [ful water].

XXI And you, blessed Maid, are you to be forgotten, given that God honoured you so much that you untied the rope which held France so tightly bound? Could one ever praise you enough for having bestowed peace on this land humiliated by war?

XXII Blessed be He who created you, Joan, who were born at a propitious hour! Maiden sent from God, into whom the Holy Spirit poured His great grace, in whom [i.e. the Holy Spirit] there was and is an abundance of noble gifts, never did Providence refuse you any request. Who can ever begin to repay you?

XXIII And what more can be said of any other person or of the great deeds of the past? Moses, upon whom God in His bounty bestowed many a blessing and virtue, miraculously and indefatigably led God's people out of Egypt. In the same way, blessed Maid, you have led us out of evil!

XXIV When we take your person into account, you who are a young maiden, to whom God gives the strength and power to be the champion who casts the rebels down and feeds France with the sweet, nourishing milk of peace, here indeed is something quite extraordinary!

XXV For if God performed such a great number of miracles through Joshua who conquered many a place and cast down many an enemy, he, Joshua, was a strong and powerful *man*. But, after all, a *woman* – a simple shepherdess – braver than any man ever was in Rome! As far as God is concerned, this was easily accomplished.

XXVI But as for us, we never heard tell of such an extraordinary marvel, for the prowess of all the great men of the past cannot be compared to this woman's whose concern it is to cast out our enemies. This is God's doing: it is He who guides her and who has given her a heart greater than that of any man.

XXVII Much is made of Gideon, who was a simple workman, and it was God, so the story tells, who made him fight; nobody could stand firm before him and he conquered everything. But whatever guidance God gave [him], it is clear that He never performed so striking a miracle as He does for this woman.

XXVIII I have heard of Esther, Judith and Deborah, who were women of great worth, through whom God delivered His people from oppression, and I have heard of many other worthy women as well, champions every one, through them He performed many miracles, but He has accomplished more through this Maid.

XXIX She was miraculously sent by divine command and conducted by the angel of the Lord to the King, in order to help him. Her achievement is no illusion for she was carefully put to the test in council (in short, a thing is proved by its effect)

XXX and well examined, before people were prepared to believe her; before it became common knowledge that God had sent her to the King, she was brought before clerks and wise men so that they could find out if she was telling the truth. But it was found in history-records that she was destined to accomplish her mission;

XXXI for more than 500 years ago, Merlin, the Sibyl and Bede foresaw her coming, entered her in their writings as someone who would put an end to France's troubles, made prophecies about her, saying that she would carry the banner in the French wars and describing all that she would achieve.

XXXII And, in truth, the beauty of her life proves that she has been blessed with God's grace – and for that reason her actions are more readily accepted as genuine. For whatever she does, she always has her eyes fixed on God, to whom she prays and whom she invokes and serves in word and deed; nowhere does her devotion ever falter.

XXXIII Oh, how clear this was at the siege of Orléans where her power was first made manifest! It is my belief that no miracle was ever more evident, for God so came to the help of His people that our enemies were unable to help each other any more than would dead dogs. It was there that they were captured and put to death.

XXXIV Oh! What honour for the female sex! It is perfectly obvious that God has special regard for it when all these wretched people who destroyed the whole Kingdom – now recovered and made safe by a woman, something that 5000 *men* could not have done – and the traitors [have been] exterminated. Before the event they would scarcely have believed this possible.

XXXV A little girl of sixteen (isn't this something quite supernatural?) who does not even notice the weight of the arms she bears – indeed her whole upbringing seems to have prepared her for this, so strong and resolute is she! And her enemies go fleeing before her, not one of them can stand up to her. She does all this in full view of everyone,

XXXVI and drives her enemies out of France, recapturing castles and towns. Never did anyone see greater strength, even in hundreds or thousands of men! And she is the supreme captain of our brave and able men. Neither Hector nor Achilles had such strength! This is God's doing: it is He who leads her.

XXXVII And you trusty men-at-arms who carry out the task and prove yourselves to be good and loyal, one must certainly make mention of you (you will be praised in every nation!) and not fail to speak of you and your valour in preference to everything else,

XXXVIII you who, in pain and suffering, expose life and limb in defence of what is right and dare to risk confronting every danger. Be constant, for this, I promise, will win you glory and praise in heaven. For whoever fights for justice wins a place in Paradise – this I do venture to say.

XXXIX And so, you English, draw in your horns for you will never capture any good game! Don't attempt any foolish enterprise in France! You have been check-mated. A short time ago, when you looked so fierce, you had no inkling that this would be so; but you were not yet treading the path upon which God casts down the proud.

XL You thought you had already conquered France and that she must remain yours. Things have turned out otherwise, you treacherous lot! Go and beat your drums elsewhere, unless you want to taste death, like your companions, whom wolves may well devour, for their bodies lie dead amidst the furrows!

XLI And know that she will cast down the English for good, for this is God's will: He hears the prayer of the good whom they wanted to harm! The blood of those who are dead and have no hope of being brought back to life again cries out against them. God will tolerate this no longer – He has decided, rather, to condemn them as evil.

XLII She will restore harmony in Christendom and the Church. She will destroy the unbelievers people talk about, and the heretics and their vile ways, for this is the substance of a prophecy that has been made. Nor will she have mercy on any place which treats faith in God with disrespect.

XLIII She will destroy the Saracens, by conquering the Holy Land. She will lead Charles there, whom God preserve! Before he dies he will make such a journey. He is the one who is to conquer it. It is there that she is to end her days and that both of them are to win glory. It is there that the whole enterprise will be brought to completion.

XLIV Therefore, in preference to all the brave men of times past, this woman must wear the crown, for her deeds show clearly enough already that God bestows more courage upon her than upon all those men about whom people speak. And she has not yet accomplished her whole mission! I believe that God bestows her here below so that peace may be brought about through her deeds.

XLV And yet destroying the English race is not her main concern for her aspirations lie more elsewhere: it is her concern to ensure the survival of the Faith. As for the English, whether it be a matter for joy or sorrow, they are done for. In days to come scorn will be heaped on them. They have been cast down!

XLVI And all you base rebels who have joined them, you can see now that it would have been better for you to have gone forwards rather than backwards as you did, thereby becoming the serfs of the English. Beware that more does not befall you (for you have been tolerated long enough!), and remember what the outcome will be!

XLVII Oh, all you blind people, can't you detect God's hand in this? If you can't, you are truly stupid for how else could the Maid who strikes you all down dead have been sent to us? – And you don't have sufficient strength! Do you want to fight against God?

XLVIII Has she not led the King with her own hand to his coronation? No greater deed was performed at Acre; for there were certainly plenty of opponents. But in spite of everyone, he was most nobly received and truly anointed, and there he heard mass.

XLIX It was exactly on the 17th day of July 1429 that Charles was, without any doubt, safely crowned at Rheims, amidst great triumph and splendour and surrounded by many men-at-arms and barons; and he stayed there for approximately five days,

L with the little Maid. As he returns through his country, neither city nor castle nor small town can hold out against them. Whether he be loved or hated, whether they be dismayed or reassured, the inhabitants surrender. Few are attacked, so fearful are they of his power.

LI It is true that some, in their folly, think they can resist, but this serves little purpose, for, in the end, whoever does offer opposition must pay God for his mistake. It is quite pointless. Whether they want to or not, they must surrender. No matter how strong the resistance offered, it collapses beneath the Maid's assault,

LII even though huge forces were gathered together, in order to launch a surprise attack and bar his return; but there is no need for a doctor's attentions now, for all his opponents have been captured and killed, one by one, and dispatched, so I've been told, to Heaven or Hell.

LIII I don't know if Paris will hold out (for they have not reached there yet) or if the Maid will delay [*or* if it will resist the Maid]. But if it decides to see her as an enemy, I fear that she will subject it to a fierce attack, as she has done elsewhere. If they offer resistance for an hour, or even half an hour, it's my belief that things will go badly for them,

LIV for /the King/ will enter Paris, no matter who may grumble about it! – The Maid has given her word that he will. Paris, do you think Burgundy will prevent him from entering? By no means, for he does not see himself as an enemy. Nobody has the power to prevent him, and you will be overcome, you and your presumption!

LV Oh Paris, how could you be so ill-advised? Foolish inhabitants, you are lacking in trust! Do you prefer to be laid waste, Paris, rather than make peace with your prince? If you are not careful your great opposition will destroy you. It would be far better for you if you were to humbly beg for mercy. You are quite miscalculating!

LVI It is the evil inhabitants I'm referring to, for there are many good people there, I have no doubt about that; but, take my word for it, these good people, who are no doubt much displeased to see their prince rejected in this way, do not dare speak out. They will not merit the punishment which will fall upon Paris and cost many a person his life.

LVII And as for you, all you rebel towns, all of you who have renounced your lord, all of you men and women who have transferred your allegiance to another, may everything now be peacefully settled, with you beseeching his pardon! For if force is used against you, the gift /i.e. of forgiveness/ will come too late [i.e. not at all, never].

LVIII And so as to avoid killing and wounding anyone [the King] delays for as long as he can, for the spilling of blood grieves him. But, in the end, if someone does not want to hand over, with good grace, what is rightly his, he is perfectly justified if he does recover it by force and bloodshed.

LIX Alas! He is so magnanimous that he wishes to pardon each and everyone. And it is the Maid, the faithful servant of God, who makes him do this. Now as loyal Frenchmen submit your hearts and yourselves to him! And when you hear him speak, you will not be reproached by anyone.

LX And I pray to God that He will prevail upon you to act in this way, so that the cruel storm of these wars may be erased from memory and that you may live your lives in peace, always loyal to your supreme ruler, so that you may never offend him and that he may be a good overlord to you. Amen.

LXI This poem was completed by Christine in the above-mentioned year, 1429, on the last day of July. But I believe that some people will be displeased by its contents, for a person whose head is bowed and whose eyes are heavy cannot look at the light.

Explicit a very beautiful poem composed by Christine.

NOTES SECTION I: VARIANTS AND REJECTED READINGS

In this section, readings in the base manuscript which have been rejected, and all our comments, are printed in italics. Berne 205 will be referred to as B, Carpentras 390 as C, Grenoble U. 909. Rés. as G.

I 1.Christienne quy C. 2.unze C. 5.fil C. 6.fuy C. 7.pour trayson C. 8.or C.

II 9.voyre de joye C. 11.quy ... soloye C. 12.gage C. 15. *line incomplete in* B. ay bon temps sy quavoir soloye C. *The reading in C seems unsatisfactory not so much because it involves a departure from the fixed rhyme scheme (cp.LVIII) as because the missing words supplied do not provide a logical link with line 16.* 16.ma per C.

III 17.CCCC et XXIX *in* C. 18.luyre le soleil C. 19.quy ramena C. 20.que on *avoit veu* B. quon ... oeul C. 21.lonc ... pluseurs C. 22.eurent vescu je suis C. 23.riens C. 24. voy *que ce* veulx B. ce que je veul C.

IV 25.sy ... ver C. 26.joye C. 28.belle *scored out before* tresbelle B. 29.sayson que prin temps C. 30.le dieu C. 31.riens C. 32.*Et est ... nee* B. sest ... tiree C. *The C reading provides a main verb for* la tresbelle saison ll.28–9.

V 33.cest que de gectie C. 35.quy lonc C. 36.*a prime* B. maintz grans ennuys quy ore aprime C. *There is a minute space between* a *and* prime in C. *If one prints* à prime, *then one must accept that there is no main verb to go with the subject* le degeté enfant l.33. *We tentatively suggest* aprime (<aprismier), *as Christine is possibly referring to the victorious approach of her King (see ll.41–2, and also our correction to the last two words of line 92).* 38.couronne C. 39.tres grandissime C. 40.*esperonne* B. et vous de or espronne C.

VI 43.resjouiz C. 44.*grans* B. menus C. 46.joye C.

VII 49.veul racompter C. 51.prie C. 52.riens C. 53.racompte C. 54.car chose ... memoyre C. 55.qui *qui* desplace B. et escripre a quy nen desplasse C. 56.coronique C.

VIII 57.oyes C. 58.toutes C. 59.nottes C. 63.sy...deceux vailable C. 64.aflati a tas C.

IX 65.*note* B. notte C. *This word, together with voie l.69, probably ought to be a second person plural imperative. Cp.* Oyez *l.57,* Notez *l.59.* 66.doibt...par C. 67.se voyant...hayr C. 68.*convint sur* B. courir sus C. *In B* convint *was clearly written in later; the scribe seems to have left a space to which he could return and write in his guess at a word or words which he did not understand in the manuscript from which he was copying.* 69.*voie* B. voye C. Cp. note on l.65. 70.*que anuit* B. quy a nuyt a maint C. *On the correction* que *to* qui, *see also ll. 103, 148, 155, though in these cases it might be possible to take* que *as a conjunction. Although* anuit *might just be acceptable (as 3rd person singular, present indicative of* ennuire, *to hurt, harm, see* J. C. Laidlaw, *The Poetical Works of Alain Chartier,* Cambridge University Press, 1974, *note on* ennuit p.449), *the word division of* C (a nuyt) *seems more plausible, since the verb* nuire *is commonly used by Christine in connection with Fortune. See, for example, Le Livre de la Mutacion de Fortune,* ed. S. Solente, Paris, Picard, vol. 2, 1959, ll.6681–3: '...pour de Fortune/ Parler, comme elle est tres commune/ De nuire aux uns...'; *and Le Livre du Chemin de Long Estude,* ed. R. Püschel, Berlin, Damköhler, Paris, Le Soudier, 1881, ll.61–4: 'Comme fortune perverse/ M'ait esté longtemps adverse/ Encor ne se puet lasser/ De moy nuire sans cesser...' *On* nuit *as a past participle, see* M. K. Pope, *From Latin to Modern French,* Manchester University Press, 1961 reprint, par. 1054. 71.*rexune* B. fais repune C. 72.quy C.

X 73.quy...advenir C. *Three letters scored out before* chose C. 74.oppinion C. 75.quy a notter C. 77.quy C. 79.mision C. 80.sy C.

XI 81.*vrayment* B. voirement C. 82.*ny ert* B. nyert nottoyre C. 84.homme...croyre C. 85.memoyre C. 87.volu...voyre C. 88.sur france *repeated and scored out* B. sy C.

XII 91.la grace quy luy donne C. 92.*la preuve* B. apert... lespreuve C. 94.*donc* B. dont...lis C. 95.que oncques B. quonques...neufve C. 96.en soy narrant la fleur de lis C.

XIII 98.septime dicelluy C. 99.quy sy...ainchoys C. 101.voy ton renom C. 103.*que* B. quy a soubzmys...pennon C.

XIV 105.len BC. 106.fust comme... imposible C. 109.*tien quique* BC. 112.quy C.

XV 113.sy C. 115.espasse C. 120.faitz C.

XVI 121.doibt C. 122.fil C. 123.quy C. 124.prophecie C. 125.s *scored out before* cerf C. 126.celluy C. 127.consome *scored out before* somme C. 128.doibt C.

XVII 129.fest le pourffit C. 130.ycelluy soyes C. 131.grief C. 132.que encores C. 133.enffans C. 134.eulx soyent C. 135.toutesvoyes C. 136.*ne guerre ny face oultre vance* B. ne guerre plus ny face oultrance C.

XVIII 138.droicturier C. 139.*tous* B. trestous aultres C. 140. que orgueil B. 141.peuple doulx C. 143.sy C.

XIX 145.porras C. 146.souffissance C. 147.faitz C. 148.*que* B. quy de sy C. 149.mys C. 150.*For this line to have eight syllables* relevee *must count as four. Cf. 185.* 151. *tresgrant sainte* providence B. ta tressainte prudence C. B *has one syllable too many.* 152.sy C.

XX 153.*Grenoble fragment begins.* loues en hault dieu C. Ah soyes loue G. 154.tenus C. 155.*que* B. quy C. qui G. 156.*ses* B. tes...advenus C. ces...advenuz G. 157. *jointes mains* B. jointtes mains tous C. a jointtes mains granz et menuz G. 158.grace...dieu C. grace...roy G. 159. quy C. 160.grand G.

XXI 161.bien euree C. en toy...bien euree G. 162.doibz... oubliee C. 163.honnouree CG. 164.*final* s *scored out after* la C. qui as...deslyee G. 165.*et estoit desliee* B. *There are dots under* des *to indicate error in* B. estroit liee C. estroit lyee G. 166.asses C. 168.as de fait paix donner C. *The* de *has been inserted above the line between* as *and* fait C. as faict paix donner G.

XXII 169.ah jehanne G. 170.benoit...quy C. 172.*esperit* B. esprit C. sainct esperit G. 173.si grand G. 175.nonque C. oncques G. 176.*que... guerredon* B. quy...asses guerdon C. qui... guerdon G.

XXIII 177.peut il estre daultre dit plus C. peult il G. 178.faitz... passes C. grands faictz du temps G. 180.vertus asses C.

181.lasses C. 182.peuple C. peuple disrael G. 183. ainsy rapasses C. 184.eslicte G.

XXIV 185.*Cf. note on 150.* considere C. puissance G. 186.quy... joyne C. joenne G. 187.quy... et renom donne C. dieu a donne povoir G. 189.quy C. mammelle G. 190.nouriture C. nourriture G. 191.rue C. a ruer G. 192.vecy... contre nature C. vecy G.

XXV 193.si... fit G. 194.sy C. 195.conquerans C. 196.en furent mais C. en furent mains G. 197.tout en somme G. 198.vecy... bregiere C. vecy... bergere G. 199.quon homs C. que homme qui... rome G.

XXVI 201.oncquez G. 202.noymes de sy grant merveilles C. ne ouysmes de si grand G. 203.lonc C. aller G. 204.quy... sa pareille C. ne sa pareille G. 205.*vaille* B. prouuesse... quy vaille C. proesse... vaille G. 206.a boute hors nos C. ennemys G. 207.quy C. 208.quy... mys C. cueur... mys G.

XXVII 209.en B. on C. fait on grand G. 210.quy C. 211.*se* dit B. fit ce dit le compte C. fit se dict le compte G. 212. combateur... narestoit C. combateur G. 213.luy CG. 214. oncques... sy C. oncquez G. 215.ny feist quoy quil lamonnestoit C. fit... ammonnestoit G. 216.cest C. comme par ceste G.

XXVIII 217.*gelbora* B. judic et dalbora C. delbora G. 218.quy C. grand G. 219.lesquelles... restaura CG. 220.*prins* B. peuple quy serf estoit pris C. peuple qui serf estoit pris G. 221.pluseurs C. plusieurs quay G. 222.quy C. premiers ny a celle G. 223.en a po *scored out before* miracles B. mais miracle en ce pourpris CG. 224.as... celle C.

XXIX 225.envoye C. envoyee G. 226.admonition C. ammonicion G. 227.langle... convoye C. convoyee G. 229.faict G. 232.effaict G.

XXX 234.ains que... volue C. aincois que on laye G. 235. clercz C. clercs et saiges G. 236.exercier... voyre C. enserсher cest chose G. 237.aincois que fust notoyre C. avant quil fust G. 238.transmise C. lavoit au roy transmise G. 239.histoyre C. en lystoire G. 240.qui dieu lavoit a ce G.

XXXI 241.merlin sebille C. par merlin sebille G. 242.V^{c} a *in* C. veirent G. 243.escript C. 244.a france C. a france... escriptz G. 245.*leur* B. leurs CG. 246.quelle porteroit C. que porteroit banniere G. 247.francoyses G. 248.faict G.

XXXII 249.vye par soy C. 251.pour C. pur quoy lon G. 252. faict G. 253.sa face G. 254.deprye G. 255.en val en place C. faict... dict G. 256.destrye G.

XXXIII 257.et comment C. comme lors bien y a paru G. 258.*orleans* B. que le siege est a orliens C. que le siege yere a orliens G. *In our printed text* siege ert *is equal to two syllables, as is* orliens. 259.du prumier C. au premier...a paru G. 260.oncques... sy con C. oncques... si comme G. 261.es siens G. 262.tellement quennemis C. tellement que ennemys G. 263.ne saidoyent C. ne se aidoient non plus que mors chiens G. 264.pris C. pris...mys G.

XXXIV 265.et C. a quel...feminin G. 266.que layme G. 267. peuple C. car tout ce grand peuple chemin G. 268.tout le *peuple* B. *The scribe has accidently copied* peuple *from the line above.* que tout le regne est C. tout le regne ere G. 269.femmes est sus C. sus G. 270.*hommes neussent* B. cent mile hommes fait neussent C. cent mil hommes neussent G. 271.traitres...en desert C. mys au desert G. 272. a paine devant main le crussent C. a paine devant nul ne creussent G.

XXXV 273.*In* G XXXV *comes immediately before* XLIV. fillette CG. 274.nest ce pas sus nature C. sur nature G. 275.quy C. 276.samble... nouriture C. nourriture G. 277.tant est forte C. forte G. 279.ne nul ne dure C. ennemys et G. 280. elle fait maint yeulx voyant C. a faict ce... voyans G.

XXXVI 281.deulx *de* france B. de eulx va france destourbant C. va france G. B *lacks finite verb.* 282.chastiaux C. 283. force ilz nont sy grant C. ilz nauront si grand G. 284. soyent...mailles C. soyent a cens soyent a mille G. 285. nos... abilles C. habiles G. 286–7 *omitted from* C. 286. est principale chevetaine G. 287.ne achilles B. ne hector narchilles G. 288.quy la mayne C. cela faict dieu qui les maine G.

XXXVII XXXVII *and* XXXVIII *not in* G. 289.esprouves C. 290. quy faittes C. 291.prouves C. 292.doibt C. 293.loues C. 294.seres C. 295.parle C.

XXXVIII 297.quy sang...vye exposes C. 298.on payne sy C. 299.perilz estes C. 300.laventure C. 301.soyes contens C. 302.aures joye au ciel et loz C. 303.droicture C. 304.gaigne...loz C.

XXXIX 305.sy rabaissies...vos C. angloys G. 306.b *scored out before* naurez B. naures biau C. 307.*mener* B. nen mener vos C. ne menez G. 308.mattes...leschaquier C. matz vous estes en leschicquier G. 309.vous *ne* pensiez B. vous ne le pensies C. pas ne le pensiez G. 310.*monstrez* B. monstries C. monstriez perillieux G. 311.nesties encore au sentier C. encores nestes au sentier G. 312. rabat C. pugnit les orgueilleux G.

XL 313.avoir france gaignie C. cuydiez...gaignee G. 314. *deult* B. deust CG. 315.faulse *mesgnie* BG. faulce mesgnie C. 316.tamborner C. aillieurs labourer G. 317.se *vos* ne B. se ne voules C. si ne voulez G. 318.vos compagnons C. 319.*povoient* B. pevent CG. 320.qua mort gissent par ces sillons C. buyssons G.

XLI 321.sachies C. saichez...angloys G. 322.mys G. 323. quy ot C. ot G. 324.*qui lont* B. quilz ont CG. 325. sang CG. 326.ne le veult plus G. 327.ains le reprouver C. le resprouver G. 328.malvais C.

XLII XLII *and* XLIII *not in* G. 329.christiente C. 331.*donc* B. dont C. 332.vye C. 333.ainsy C.

XLIII 337.sarrasins C. 338.saincte C. 339.mourra...gart C. 340.meure...cel C. 341.sil est cil quy la doibt C. 342. doibt...vye C. 343.lung...gloyre C. 344.assouvye C.

XLIV 345.*de sur* B. dont dessus...passes C. dont dessus G. 346.doibt C. 347.faitz...moustrent asses C. faictz nous monstrent G. 348.luy CG. 349.len BC. ceulx C. ceulx dont lon raisonne G. 350.*nas* B. na C. encore *written in above word scored out after* pas C. elle na pas encores G. 351.jus *leur donne* B. sy croy...jus la donne C. je croy que ca jus dieu la donne G. 352.affin C. affin...faict G.

XLV 353.est *scored out before* ait B. *quaffaire ait* B. sy... moyns qua faire ait C. cest...que a faire y ait G. 354. destruyre danglescherie G. 355.car ailleurs elle a plus son C. aillieurs plus hault hait G. 357.*que qui* B. qui que C. angloys qui que sen rye G. 358.*au parler* B. ou pleure CG. 359.advenir CG. mocquerie G.

XLVI 361.roupieux C. ruppieux G. 362.quy a eulx... allies C. 363.or voyes... que vous fust mieulx C. ne vees vous G. 364.estre allez G. 365.demourer... serfz C. angloys serfz G. 366.gardes C. advieigne G. 367.trop este aves C. 368.*bien souviengne* B. bien vous C. bien vous souvieigne G.

XLVII 369.naperceves C. ne appercepvez... aveugle G. 370. yssy C. 371.vugle C. qui ne le voit il... bugle G. 372. comme... guyse G. 373.*sa* tramise B. ycy transmise C. cy transmise G. 374.quy... mortz C. faict... abbatre G. 375. ne force *avez* B. quy force naves quy souffice C. et force navez qui suffise G. 376.voules C.

XLVIII 377.Na *elle* B. na elle mene le roy au sacre C. ja elle mene le roy G. *Correct* elle *to* el, *which occurs in line 246.* 378. quelle tient ades C. tenoit ades G. 379.plus grant oncques C. oncques si grande chose G. 380.fut faitte C. faicte G. 381.contredis y eut C. contredictz G. 382.malgre C. grand G. 383.fut receu CG. 384.oyt C.

XLIX B *has 7 lines only*: *lines* 385–7 *as printed, followed by*: du mois de juillet sauf et sains/ droit ou XVIIe jour/ ou gens darmes et barons mains/ et la fu V jours a sejour. C *has 7 lines only*: *lines* 385–7 *as printed (but with orthographical variations* fut, m^{le} iiii^{c}.), *followed by*: du mois de jullet sauf et sains/ droit o XVII jour/ a gens darmes et barons maintz/ et la fut V jours a sejour. G *has the complete stanza*: a tresgrand triumphe et puissance/ fut le roy couronne a rains/ lan mil quatre cens sans doubtance/ et XXIX tout saulf et sains/ avecques des barons mains/ droit le XXVe jour/ de juillet pou plus ou pou mains/ par cinq jours fut la a sejour. *It will be seen that* G *allows one to reconstruct* 388 *and* 391 *and to restore the penultimate line in* B *to its proper position.* In 392, *we have adopted* par *from* G, *as this provides a more logical link with* pou plus ou pou mains, which cannot apply to Droit ou XVIIe jour/ De juillet.

L 393.*pucelle* B. avec luy la pucellette C. avecquez luy la pucellette G. 394.vers son pays C. pays G. 395.ne *inserted above the line between* cite *and* chastel B. chastiau C. cite chasteau ne aultre villette G. 396.ames ne hays C. aymez G. 397.qui ne soit ou soyent esbays G. 398.

asseures C. et mesmement les G. 399.peu son envais C. sans estre envahys G.

LI 401.que aucuns B. quaucuns C. combien que aucuns de leur folye G. 402.cuydent... pou G. 403.*qui que* contralie B. desrain qui contralie C. *Line repeated with variations in* C: quy contrarie. 404.*Word scored out before* dieu *in* C. compare G. 405.nyent G. 406.veullent... sy C. 407.quy C. resistence G.

LII 409.en B. quoy quon ayt... assamblee C. quoy quon ayt faict G. 410.cuydant G. 411.luy courir sus C. luy courir sur G. 412.myre C. vault confort ne mire G. 413.mortz C. 414. contredis C. contredictz G. 415.envoye comme C. envoyez comme jay ouy dire G. 416.*End of Grenoble fragment.*

LIII 418.encore... mye C. 420.ennemye C. 421.*or* estrenne? B. *The loop of the* s *makes it very difficult to distinguish whether the third letter in the word is* t *or* c. *The rhyme-scheme calls for* escremie. doubte... estraine C. 422.luy... sy C. 423.sil resiste... demye C. 424.yra se croy C.

LIV 425.quy... grongne C. 426.luy C. 427.bourgoigne C. 428. deffendis... mys C. 430.*nul nest* B. nul na puissance C. 431.quy... et en soubz mis C. 432.segas et toute oultrecuidance C.

LV 433.o pais C. 435.*ayme* BC. exillie C. 436.acordance C. 439.fust C.

LVI 441.*gens a dedens* mauvais B. jentens des malvais cas C. 442.fay C. 444.*moult desplaist et* sans B. moult il desplait sans C. 445.ainsy C. 447.sa boute C. 448.paris et... vye C.

LVII 450.quy aves renye C. 452.quy... aultre laves nye C. 453. ades aplanye C. 454.requerans C. 455.*este* B. estes magnie C. 456.*ou* don B. par force... vendres a don C.

LVIII 457.*qui* B. quil C. 458.faitte il retarde... peut C. 459. cher domme C. *Word scored out before* incision C. 462. que est B. quest C. 464.*la requerra il fut* B. le recouvre il fait C.

LIX 465.hellas il est sy de bonnayre C. 467.luy C. 468.quy C. 469.veullies vos cuers a vous C. 470.loyalz . . . luy C. 471. vauldra C. 472.ne seres repris C.

LX 473.sy prie . . . mette C. 474.facies C. 475.*conseil* B. affin que le cruel C. 476.effacies C. 477.passies. 478.gregneur C. 479.*leffaciez* B. loffensies C. 480.*bien* B. quenvers . . . bon segneur C.

LXI 481.dictie . . . christiene C. 482.dessus m^{le} iiii^{c} *in* C. 484. jullet C. 485.que aucuns B. quaulcuns C. 486.de ce quy contient C. 487.embronchee et ses yeulx grans C. 488. peut C. *The signature* Henry de Castellane *is visible after the Explicit in* C.

NOTES SECTION II: LITERARY, HISTORICAL AND LINGUISTIC NOTES

I In the first *huitain* Christine refers to a number of events which took place in 1418 i.e. the Burgundian occupation of Paris on 29 May ('la traïson' l.7), the Dauphin's escape (l.6) and her own flight to the safety of an 'abbaye close' (l.2, l.7). In 1418 France was still faced with the twin problems of foreign invasion and civil strife between Armagnacs and Burgundians. On Sunday 29 May 1418, Perrinet Leclerc, the son of a 'marchand de fer' in Paris who kept the keys of the Porte Saint-Germain-des-Prés, opened the city gates to the Burgundians, thus securing his revenge for harsh treatment meted out to him by some Armagnac soldiers and for the failure of the prévôt de Paris, Tanneguy du Chastel, to deal with his complaint. The Dauphin's flight, which left Charles VI and the whole of northern France to Burgundian domination, is described as follows in the chronicle of Jean Juvénal des Ursins: 'Messire Tanneguy du Chastel oüyt le bruit, et s'en vint hastivement en l'hostel de monseigneur le Dauphin, lequel dormoit en son lict: et ainsi que Dieu le voulut, le prit entre ses bras, l'enveloppa de sa robbe à relever, et le porta à la Bastille de Sainct Antoine. Là le fit habiller, et le mena jusques à Melun' (Michaud et Poujoulat, *Nouvelle Collection de Mémoires relatifs à l'Histoire de France*, Paris, Didier, vol. 2, 1857, p. 540). There followed a general massacre in Paris which claimed some 2000 of the Dauphin's supporters. For some miniatures showing the Burgundians entering Paris and the consequent massacre, see Françoise du Castel, *Damoiselle Christine de Pizan*, Paris, Picard, 1972, p. CV and p. CVII.

l.2. *abbaye close*. For the possibility that this may have been the Dominican convent at Poissy, where Christine's daughter had taken orders c. 1396, see Introduction p.2. Among the nuns at Poissy was the Dauphin's own sister, Marie de France (see Vallet de Viriville, 'Notes sur l'état civil des princes et des princesses nés de Charles VI et d'Isabeau de Bavière', *Bibliothèque de l'Ecole des Chartes*, 19, DIV, 1858, pp. 473–482, and Y. Grandeau, 'Les Enfants de Charles VI', *Bulletin philologique et historique* 1967, ii, pp. 809–849). Her presence in the convent, combined with Christine's ever-alert interest in political affairs, might explain why Christine seems so well-informed in the *Ditié* as to the day-to-day course of events in 1429.

l.5 *se dire l'ose.* When she 'dares' to refer to Charles as the King's son, what Christine has in mind is not the alleged illegitimacy of Charles VII but the fact that Anglo-Burgundian pressure had forced Charles VI to disinherit the Dauphin by the Treaty of Troyes, 21 May 1420, and to recognise Henry V of England as his son and rightful heir to the French throne.

l.7. *enclose* refers to Christine l.1.

II l.10 *yvernage*. Misreadings (on the part of the nineteenth-century editors of the poem) of the initial letter y of *yvernage* as the letter p accompanied by a sign indicating an abbreviation for *por/pour* resulted in the word *vernage* appearing in Godefroy, where it is glossed as a noun meaning 'printemps'. Godefroy's one recorded example of *vernage* = *spring* must therefore be rejected. For a fuller discussion of *vernage*, see Angus J. Kennedy and Kenneth Varty, '*Vernage*: Two Corrections to Godefroy', *Medium Aevum*, XLIV, 2, 1975, pp. 162–3.

IV l.32. (*la tresbelle saison*) ... *S'est du sec au vert temps tirée.* Although the manuscript readings may be corrupt here, the general meaning seems clear: lit. 'the beautiful season ... has drawn away from the dry to the green time' i.e. 'winter has given way to spring'.

V l.33. The Dauphin had been disinherited by the Treaty of Troyes, 21 May 1420 (see note on l.5) and by a decision of the Paris *parlement* in January 1421 (see M.G.A. Vale, *Charles VII*, London, Eyre Methuen, 1974, p.32).

l.34. *roy de France legitime*: Charles VI, who had died on 21 October 1422.

l.37. *ainsi que vers prime*: lit. 'as if towards prime' i.e. 'like one rising up to go to prime'.

l.39. *tresgrande*: In the *Ditié* there are more old feminine forms without –e than there are analogical forms with –e. On *grant* as a feminine form, see 88, 99, 117, 148, 160, 173, 202, 283, 379, 382, 409, 437; *tel* 113, 150, 287, 372 (contrast *telement* 262); *fort* 277 (contrast *forte* 406); *preux* 199 (contrast *preuses* 222).

VI l.48. *en hault huer*. Although perhaps best translated into English by 'in a loud voice', *huer* is the infinitive form (=to shout), and belongs to the sequence introduced by *Alons* in l.44: '*Alons trestous ... le saluer ... en hault huer*'.

VII l.55. *Et escript: soit* has obviously to be understood after *escript* (compare *Raconté soit* l.53).

IX l.71. *repune*. A scribal error in Berne 205, reproduced in the nineteenth-century editions of the poem, explains the presence of *rexune* in Godefroy where it is glossed as a noun meaning 'crainte' (sub. *resoigne*). *Rexune* like *vernage*, therefore, (see above, II, l.10) is a ghost-word whose appearance is based on misreadings. The correct reading (in Carpentras) is *repune*, 3 person singular, present tense of *repugnier, repuner*.

X ll.73–84 provide a clear illustration of the way in which Christine's syntax reflects the tortuous complexity of the Latin period. l.79. *mission* here seems to be close to its etymological sense: 'act of sending'.

XI l.87. *adès*. Although single *adès* is sometimes glossed as 'now', its basic meaning is 'always'. Professor T.B.W. Reid has drawn our attention to the possibility that *adès* in l.87 may have the sense of 'nevertheless'— a sense derived from the basic meaning 'always'.

XII l.96. i.e. French Kings have always been good Christians.

XIII–XIV These two *huitains* illustrate the readiness with which Christine dislocates the expected verse-pattern: the two words forming the conjunction *ainçois que* (ll.99–100) are separated at the rhyme, the expected pause at the end of *huitain* XIII is ignored, the adverb *visiblement* is split into two parts, at the rhyme. For other examples of this latter point, see *Livre de la Mutacion de Fortune ed.cit.* vol. 2 ll.7276–7:... 'de savoir entiere–/Ment cognoistre les choses belles...'; ll.7352–3: 'Ce est disputer autentique–/ Ment contre vices et pechiez.'; and vol.3 ll.17541–2: 'Riche sepulture parfaicte–/ Ment belle...'.

XV l.119 is probably to be taken as the second *que* clause introduced by *Si croy* of l.113. The switch to the subjunctive in l.119 need not be taken to imply a degree of doubt, particularly when the clause is so distant from the main verb. Marie-Josèphe Pinet points out (*op.cit.* p.446 note 2) that E. Müller's thesis *Zur Syntax der Christine de Pisan* (diss. Greifswald 1885) draws attention to Christine's very frequent use of the subjunctive.

XVI Predictions that Charles VII would go on to ever-greater victories and achievements were naturally wide-spread in 1429 – see, for example, a reference to such predictions in the letter of 10 May 1429 reported in the *Chronique d' Antonio Morosoni*: 'On n'a cessé de parler de beaucoup de prophéties trouvées à Paris et d'autres choses qui s'accordent pour annoncer que le dauphin doit grandement prospérer' (ed. L. Dorez et G. Lefèvre-Pontalis, Paris, Renouard, 1898–1902, 4 vols., *Société de l'Histoire de France*, vol. 3, pp. 39–41). The specific prophecy contained in *huitain* XVI that a French King would arise who would surpass all monarchs and one day become Emperor was one that was long-established and continually revived, giving expression as it did to French nationalist aspirations. It was probably given its widest currency in the works of Jean de Roque-Taillade (mid-fourteenth century) and in the so-called 'Second Charlemagne' prophecy associated with Telesphorus of Cosenza in the 1380s – a prophecy that may well have influenced the conclusion of Christine's *Livre du Chemin de Long Estude* (1403), where she looks forward to the transfer of Imperial power to France (*Livre du Chemin de Long Estude ed. cit.* ll.6251–6262 and Pinet *op.cit.* p. 198 note 1 and p. 301). On Jean de Roque-Taillade and Telesphorus of Cosenza, and the whole question of political prophecy, see Marjorie Reeves, *The Influence of Prophecy in the Later Middle Ages. A study in Joachimism,* Oxford, Clarendon Press, 1969, particularly Part III, chapter III 'The Second Charlemagne'; Migne, *Nouvelle Encyclopédie Théologique,* vol. 24: *Dictionnaire des Prophéties et des Miracles,* 2 tomes, Paris, 1852, tome 2, col. 690, *Prophéties politiques.*

l.125. 'Le Cerf Volant'. While the emblem of the Cerf Volant goes back to the reign of Charles V (see, for example, Lord Howard de Walden, *Banners Standards and Badges from a Tudor Manuscript in the College of Arms,* the de Walden Library, London, 1904, p.53 and Paul Delaunay, *La Zoologie au seizième siècle,* Paris, Hermann, 1962 (Histoire de la Pensée VII), p.38), two main traditions regarding the origins of *Le Cerf Volant* as an emblem or symbol of the French King date to the reign of Charles VI. Jean Juvénal des

Ursins, basing himself on the *Chronique du Religieux de Saint Denis*, relates the emblem to an encounter between Charles VI and a stag in the forest of Senlis, in 1380: 'Et de là s'en alla à Senlis pour chasser. Et fut trouvé un cerf qui avoit au col une chaisne de cuivre doré, et defendit qu'on ne le prit que au las, sans le tuer, et ainsi fut fait. Et trouva-on qu'il avoit au cou ladite chaisne, où avoit escrit: *Caesar hoc mihi donavit.* Et dès lors le Roy de son mouvement porta en devise le cerf volant couronné d'or au col, et partout où on mettoit ses armes y avoit deux cerfs tenans ses armes d'un costé et d'autre' (Michaud et Poujoulat, *Nouvelle Collection de Mémoires relatifs à l'Histoire de France,* vol. 2, Paris, Didier, 1857, pp.343–4. Compare *Chronique du Religieux de Saint Denis* 1, p.71, in *Collection de Documents inédits sur l'histoire de France,* vol. 6, Paris, Crepelet, 1839). Froissart, by contrast, relates the emblem to one of Charles VI's dreams. At Senlis, Charles VI dreams that he is in the city of Arras, where the Count of Flanders presents him with a magnificent falcon. Whilst out hunting, Charles loses sight of the falcon and is afraid that he will never set eyes on it again. 'En che sousi que li rois avoit, ly estoit vis que uns trop biaux chers douse, et à elles, apparoit à yaulx en yssant hors de ce fort bois, et venoit en celle lande et s'enclinoit devant le roy; et li rois dissoit au connestable qui regardoit ce cerf à mervelles et en avoit grant joie: 'Connestables, demorés ychy; je monteray sus che cerf qui se représente à moy, et sievray mon faucon'. Charles is then borne aloft by the stag and soon recovers his falcon. 'Adont s'esvilloit li rois, et avoit grant mervelle de celle vission, et trop bien li souvenoit de tout ce, et le recorda à aucuns de ceulx de sa cambre qui le plus prochain de li estoient, et tant li plaissoit li figure de che cerf que à paines en ymaginations il n'en pooit partir, et fu li une des incidenses premiers quant il descendy en Flandre combatre les Flamens, pour quoy le plus il encarga en sa devise le cerf-vollant à porter' (*Oeuvres de Froissart,* ed. Kervyn de Lettenhove, tome 10, pp. 68–71, Réimpression de l'édition de 1867–77, Biblio Verlag, Osnabrück, 1967). Whatever the exact origins of the emblem, it is clear that long before the date of composition of the *Ditié* the Cerf Volant had become a well-established representative symbol of the French King (see, for example, Deschamps, *Oeuvres Complètes* ed. Marquis de Queux de Saint Hilaire et Gaston Raynaud, Paris, Firmin Didot, 1878–1903, *Société des Anciens Textes Français,* vol. 1, p. 164, *Balade* LXVII; Philippe de Mezières, *Le Songe du Vieil Pelerin,* ed. G. W. Coopland, Cambridge University Press, 1962, 2 vols., where the author frequently refers to Charles VI as the Cerf Volant. The Frontispiece of vol. 2 shows a representation of the Cerf Volant, from Arsenal Ms. 2682–3, fol. 34r). It is worth pointing out too that the encounter between Charles VI and a stag with a collar bearing the inscription *Caesar hoc mihi donavit* (as described in Juvénal des Ursins' version) provides another reminder of the claim that the French King's saw themselves as the true heirs of the Roman Emperors.

XVII l.136. Presumably *guerre* is the subject, *oultrance* the noun object of *face*, lit. 'let not war cause excess i.e. havoc, destruction'. One could perhaps consider emending *face* to *face*[*s*], take *guerre* to be the object, and *oultrance* to be the equivalent of Modern French *à outrance* i.e. 'May you never wage war to the death!' A second person singular verb (*faces*) certainly provides a more logical link with l.135.

XVIII Christine's portrait of the ideal monarch is much influenced by her admiration for Charles V (see her biography of Charles V, *Livre des fais et bonnes meurs du sage roy Charles V* ed. S. Solente, Paris, Champion, 2 vols., 1936 and 1941, or the chapters on 'le bon prince' in the *Livre du Corps de Policie* and the *Livre de la Paix*.

l.143. *premisse*. Professor T.B.W. Reid has made the following comment on this word: 'The only attested words this could represent are *premices* 'first-fruits', nearly always in the plural, and *premisse* 'premiss' (in logic), also 'foreword, beginning'. It seems likely enough that these two words might have tended to coalesce and be confused; and the meaning here may be something like 'first sample' or 'first manifestation''.

XXII ll.172–5: In spite of the apparent parallelism between *En qui* 172 and *en qui* 173, it is probable that the second *qui* refers not to *Pucelle* 171 but to the *Saint Esprit* 172.

XXIII l.179. *Moÿses*. The allusions to the heroes and heroines of the Old testament (Moses 179, Joshua 193, Gideon 209, Esther, Judith, Deborah 217) are clearly designed to show that the 'miracle' of Joan surpasses all previous manifestations of God's grace and power.

l.179. *afflus*. This is a rare word, which is not recorded in Godefroy or Tobler-Lommatzsch. Some editors have taken *afflus* to be a noun (e.g. Fabre glosses the word as *abondance*). *Afflus* is in fact an adjective (from Latin *adfluus*, *afluus*, glossed in Du Cange under *affluitas* as *abundans*), translatable in this context by 'bountiful' or 'in His bounty'. Cp. also the *Thesavrvs Lingvae Latinae* (aditvs avctoritate et consilio academiarvm qvinqve Germanicarvm, Lipsiae, MDCCCC, vol. 1), under *afluus*, where one example is given, from Julius Valerius: 'flumen. . .adfluum vident'.

XXV ll.193–7. *Josué.* Joshua was Moses' successor as leader of the Israelites, his main achievement being the conquest of the land of Canaan. The most celebrated miracle associated with him is the halting of the sun which allowed him to complete his victory over the Amorites (*Joshua* 10, 12–14).

XXVI ll.203–5 provide a clear example of an elliptical, mid-sentence change of grammatical construction by which Christine conveys breathless excitement at Joan's achievement.

l.203. *au long aler*: the usual meaning of this expression in Christine's works is 'after a long time'. See, for example, *Livre de la Mutatacion de Fortune ed.cit.*, vol.4, p.190, under *aler.* Its probable meaning in l.203 i.e. 'throughout history' can be seen as an extension of its basic sense: 'after a long time', 'in the course of time', 'throughout history'.

XXVII l.209. *Gedeon*: Like Joan, Gideon was entrusted with a divinely-ordained mission to deliver his country from oppression. On his conquest of the Midianites, see *Judges*, chapters 6–8.

ll.214–6: l.215 raises a number of problems: the exact meaning of *ammonestoit*, the use of the indicative after *quoy que* (to be understood as 'although' or 'whatever'?), the identity of *il* (God or Gideon?) and the fact that the C reading includes an object pronoun (*quoy qu'il l' ammonestoit*). We have taken the possible meanings of 214–6 to be: 'But whatever guidance He (God) did in fact give [him = Gideon]' or 'Although He (God) did in fact guide [him = Gideon], it is clear that He never performed so striking a miracle as He does for this woman'.

XXVIII l.217. *Hester, Judith et Delbora.* As female embodiments of the spirit of courage and self-sacrifice, Esther, Judith and Deborah inevitably occupy a prominent place in a

number of Christine's works, notably in the *Cité des Dames* and in the *Livre de la Mutacion de Fortune*. What these three great heroines of Biblical history have in common is the fact that they, like Joan, were chosen to be the servants of God and entrusted with the special task of delivering their nation from oppression. Esther's defeat of Haman's plot against the Jews is related in *Esther*, chapters 6–7, Judith's victory over Holofernes in *Judith*, chapters 8–16, Deborah's overthrow of Sisera at the Battle of Kishon in *Judges*, chapters 4–5. De Roche and Wissler suggest that the 'Song of Deborah' (*Judges* 5) may in fact have influenced the composition of the *Ditié*: 'Les ressemblances entre ce chant et celui de Christine nous font supposer que le premier a inspiré la conception du second. Il y a d'abord une analogie de faits dans la situation politique des deux peuples, israélite et français: affaiblissement général de l'ordre politique par la discorde intérieure; indépendance du pays menacée par les envahisseurs, là les Canaanéens, ici les Anglais; appel aux armes des prophétesses, Débora, Jeanne; confiance des chefs, Barac, Charles VII ou Dunois; intervention et secours inattendus de Dieu dans la bataille; victoire et triomphe. Dans les deux chants domine la louange de Dieu '(*Festschrift Louis Gauchat*, Aarau, 1926, p.351. Cp. Fabre *ed.cit.* tome 2, pp.330–338). De Roche and Wissler then go on to draw attention to what they regard as a number of similarities in manner as well as in matter: *Ditié* LV–LVI cp. Judges 5, 2–3, for the image of the storm *Ditié* XX cp. *Judges* 5, 4–5, for the image of light *Ditié* LXI cp. *Judges* 5, 31.
Comparison between Joan and these three Biblical heroines in particular must have become commonplace at a very early date – see, for example, the note on Joan added to a manuscript of the *Breviarium historiale* in 1429, Fabre *ed.cit.* pp. 318–9, and Gerson's treatise mentioned in our introduction p.11.

l.222. *Qui furent preuses, n'y ot celle.* Professor T.B.W. Reid has suggested that *n'y ot celle* has probably to be seen as an elliptical construction equivalent to 'there is not one who is not' and translatable by 'everyone of them'. See Tobler-Lommatzsch I, 770, and II, 90–91 and Tobler's *Vermischte Beiträge* I, 3rd ed., 137.

XXIX ll.227–8. The date of Joan's arrival at Chinon is traditionally given as 6 March, 1429. It may, however, have been earlier, possibly 22 February. See Régine Pernoud, *Joan of Arc*, Penguin Books, 1964, p.47.

XXX ll.233–240 (and ll.230–33 of XXIX) refer to the interrogation to which Joan was subjected at Poitiers, March–April 1429.

ll.233–4: The *a* of l.234 is the auxiliary in post-position (*bien esté examinée a*). Cp. *Livre du Chemin de Long Estude ed.cit.*: 'Jadis Remus et Romulus/Qui à leur mere esté tollus/Orent par leur oncle crueux...' (ll.3577–9), and *Livre de la Mutacion de Fortune ed.cit.* vol. 3, ll.18275–6: '...tant esté menez/orent de tempeste...'.

XXXI l.241. *Merlin et Sebile et Bede.* In this *huitain* Christine is referring to a number of prophecies which were circulating at the time and which were applied to Joan once she had embarked on her mission. A prophecy attributed to Merlin in Geoffrey of Monmouth's *Historia Regum Britanniae* ('Ex nemore canuto puella eliminabitur ut medelae curam adhibeat') was popularly taken to refer to Joan, 'ex nemore canuto' being interpreted as 'from the Bois-Chenu' of Domrémy. Joan herself seems to have been aware of this prediction (see Quicherat, *op.cit.* 1, p.68). At the Trial of Rehabilitation (1450–56) Merlin's prophecy was referred to briefly by Pierre Miget (Quicherat *op.cit.* 3, p.133) and discussed in detail by Jean Bréhal (Quicherat *op.cit.* 3, pp.339–344). For allusions to Merlin's prophecies in two fifteenth-century chronicles, the *Registre Delphinal* and the *Scotichronicon*, see Quicherat *op.cit.*, 4, p.305, p.480. *Sebile* requires no special comment as throughout the Middle Ages a host of predictions were given the prestige of the Sibyl's authority. *Bede*: Although it might at first sight appear odd to find the Venerable Bede mentioned alongside Merlin and the Sibyl, the three were in fact often associated in the Middle Ages – indeed Merlin and Bede were not only associated but often confused with each other (see *Chronique d'Antonio Morosoni* ed.cit. vol.4, p.319). A chronogram attributed to Bede and pointing to 1429 was circulating in Paris in that same year. One version of it appears in an Italian letter of 9 July 1429, written from Bruges to Venice (*Chronique d'Antonio Morosoni ed.cit.* vol.3, p.127: 'A Paris...il a été trouvé mout prophéties qui font mention de cette damoiselle, entre lesquels il y en a une de Bède...'). At the Trial of Rehabilitation the Bede prophecy was discussed by Jean Bréhal (Quicherat *op.cit.* 3, pp.338–9). For a general discussion of the prophecies attributed to Bede and Merlin, see Andrew Lang, *The Maid of France*, London, Longmans Green, 1909, pp.32–3, 145, 308–311 and *Chronique d' Antonio Morosoni ed.cit.* vol.4, Annexe xvi, pp.316–327.

XXXIII l.258. Joan raised the siege of Orléans on 8 May 1429.

l.263. *ne que mors chiens.* This is an elliptical construction translatable by 'no more than would dead dogs [help each other]'.

XXXIV On the feminist theme articulated in this stanza, see our introduction pp.15–16. Ironically, at her trial Joan was to be accused of having dishonoured her sex (see Quicherat *op.cit.*, 1, p.223).

ll.267–71. The main verb for the subjects of the *Quant* clause (*ce grant pueple chenin* and *les traictres*) is understood i.e. [have been] *mis à desert*; l.269 should be seen as a parenthesis, referring to *le regne* of l.268.

XXXVI l.287. Christine's gently ironic comment that the achievements of a mere 'fillete de XVI ans' surpass those of Hector and Achilles should of course be linked to the feminist theme running right through the poem.

XXXVII ll.292–6: a rather convoluted sentence whose structure is not immediately apparent: 'on en doit faire mention et [on doit] parler de vous'...

l.295. *sur toute election* lit. 'over every choice' i.e. 'in preference to everything else'. Cp. the expression *sur toute rien.*

XLI l.322 *sans relever* and l.325 *sans lever.* We take *sans relever* and *sans lever* to be synonyms, meaning 'without rising up' i.e. 'well and truly dead'. (Fabre, by contrast, glosses *sans lever* as *sans relâche ed.cit.* p.323). On *lever= se lever, relever= se relever*, see Godefroy 4,768b and 6,764a. One of the examples given by Godefroy is rather similar to the ones in the *Ditié*: 'Ja peussiez veoir brisier lances et chevaliers cheoir *sans relever*'.

l.327. *ains les reprouver*: 'rather [does He wish] to condemn them'.

XLII–III In these two *huitains* belief in Joan's universal mission combines with the 'Second Charlemagne' prophecy (referred to in note on XVI) which predicted not only the transfer of Imperial power to France but also the restoration of the Church, the new Emperor's liberation of the Holy Land and his eventual death there.

ll.329–333. Although the Council of Constance had formally brought an end to the Great Schism (1378–1417), it did not in practice remove the divisions and tensions within Western Christendom. A clear indication of continuing strife is given in l.332 where Christine refers to the Hussites who had embarked on a savage war of revenge after the arrest, imprisonment and burning of John Huss as a heretic on 6 July 1415. For a letter to the Hussites (wrongly) attributed to Joan, see Quicherat *op.cit.* 5, pp.156–9. As well as having to cope with internal strife, Christendom was still facing the continual assault of the Turks (the *mescreans* referred to in l.331).

ll.337–339: That Joan herself may have envisaged a Crusade is indicated in two letters, the first to the King of England, the Duke of Bedford and others, written on 22 March 1429: 'Vous, duc de Bedford, la Pucelle vous prie et vous requiert que vous ne vous faictes mie destruire. Se vous lui faictes raison, encore pourrez venir en sa compaignie, l'où que les Franchois feront le plus bel fait que oncques fu fait pour la chrestienté' (Quicherat *op.cit.* 1, p.241). In her letter to the Duke of Burgundy, dated 17 July 1429, she wrote: 'Hault et redoubté prince, duc de Bourgoingne, Jehanne la Pucelle vous requiert de par le Roy du ciel, mon droicturier et souverain seigneur, que le Roy de France et vous, faciez bonne paix ferme, qui dure longuement. Pardonnez l'un à l'autre de bon cuer, entièrement, ainsi que doivent faire loyaulx chrestians; et s'il vous plaist à guerroier, si alez sur les Sarrazins' (Quicherat *op.cit.* 5, p.126).

ll.339–341: as indicated above, the prediction that a French monarch-Emperor would be present at the liberation of the Holy Land was wide-spread. 'Partout au XVe siècle', points out Maurice Chaume, 'on croit qu'un roi de France va surgir, qui ceindra la couronne impériale, réformera l'Eglise, battra le Turc, et s'en ira mourir à Jérusalem' (*Revue du Moyen Age Latin*, iii, 1947, p.36).

XLV l.354. *L'Englecherie*. This word is used here by Christine to refer pejoratively to the whole English race and all that it stands for. The only example Godefroy gives of this particular usage is the one which occurs in the *Ditié*. *Englecherie* was a term which originally had a legal connotation. In Norman England the 'presentment of Englishry' (i.e. the offering of proof that a slain person was English) was a method whereby a community could escape the fine which would automatically be levied in the event of a Norman being murdered. Even in its original legal sense in Norman England, therefore the word had pejorative overtones.

l.356. Like ll.329–344, this line reflects an already firmly-established belief in Joan's universal mission.

l.358. Fabre *ed.cit.* p.325 translates *il en est sué* by 'maintenant on en est débarrassé', while Buchon *ed.cit.* p.542 suggests 'Décrété ainsi'. The context seems to suggest that the meaning may be 'it's all up with them', although one would like additional evidence apart from the context to confirm this.

XLVI l.361. Christine is referring here to the Burgundians in particular.

XLVIII l.379. *Acre*: the capture of Acre in 1191 during the Third Crusade led by Philip Augustus and Richard Lion-Heart.

XLIX l.392. Charles and Joan arrived at Rheims on 16 July and left on 21 July 1429. Line 392 provides yet another indication of how well-informed Christine was on the day-to-day movements of Charles' army.

L l.395. The French troops were at Vailly on 22 July, at Soissons on 23, at Château-Thierry on 29 July 1429.

l.396. *remaint*. *Remaindre/remanoir* in this kind of context normally needs a phrase or complement cp. *Roland* 1.4 'N'i ad castel ki *devant lui* remaigne' and *Livre du Chemin de Long Estude ed.cit.* ll.3674–9: 'Et comment puet-ce estre/

Qu'ainsi ses bons en Alemaigne/Fait a present, qu'il ne remaigne/Ville, chastel, pais ne bourc/En la duchié de Lucembourc/*Qui ne lui viengne faire* hommage?' 'Devant lui' or 'devant elle' should probably therefore be understood in l.396. Alternatively, one could adopt the following suggestion from Professor T.B.W. Reid: 'The usual construction would be with a dependent clause of the type *que ne se rende*; and I suspect that this is the underlying idea here, though it has been overlaid (as happens not infrequently in Old French) by the corresponding affirmative principal clause, *les habitans se rendent*'. If this suggestion were adopted, one would require to repunctuate (replace full stop after *remaint* by a comma) and link the two clauses (395–6, 398–99) by a 'but that' construction in English (literally: 'not a city remains but that its inhabitants surrender'.).

l.400. *Sa* could be taken to refer either to Joan or Charles.

LIII ll.417–9. Christine's doubts as to whether Paris would resist or not suggests she was aware of the negotiations between Charles VII and the Duke of Burgundy, whose envoys had arrived in Rheims on the very day of Charles' coronation. The Duke of Burgundy was of course simply playing for time, in order to allow John, Duke of Bedford, to fortify Paris in preparation for the expected assault (see Vallet de Viriville, *Histoire de Charles VII*, vol.2, Paris, Renouard, 1863, pp. 101–2).

l.419. *attendra.* The subject of *attendra* could be either *Paris* (with *Pucelle* as object) or *la Pucelle*; both possibilities give acceptable sense: (a) 'or if it will resist the Maid' (see Tobler-Lommatzsch I, 631–2) or (b) 'or if the Maid will delay' (cp. l. 458).

l.422. The subject of *rende* and *a fait* is *she* (Joan) understood.

l.424. *Son* refers to Paris, though the subject of the sentence is plural *ilz* (i.e. the inhabitants of Paris); *fait*= state, condition. Fabre *ed.cit.* p.327 takes *son* to refer to Joan and translates *de son fait* by 'grâce à elle'. For Fabre's suggestion to be plausible, one would really require 'par son fait' cp. l. 352.

LIV l.425. The subject of l.425 is Charles VII understood.

ll.425–6. Neither Joan's nor Christine's optimism turned out to be well-founded: the attack on Paris on 8 September 1429 failed, Joan was captured at Compiègne on 23 May 1430, handed over to the English and burned as a heretic in Rouen on 30 May 1431. Charles VII was not to enter Paris till 12 November 1437, having eventually reconciled himself with the Duke of Burgundy by the Treaty of Arras, 20 September 1435.

l.426. Modern French would require the direct pronoun *le* to be stated.

l.427. *Bourgoingne*: i.e. Philippe le Bon, who had become Duke of Burgundy in 1419, after the assassination of his father, Jean sans Peur.

ll.429–30. The subject of *non fera* is 'the Duke of Burgundy' understood. 'The Duke of Burgundy will not do this i.e. prevent Charles from entering Paris'. The omission of the subject pronoun produces an ambiguity in the next part of the same sentence re. he/his: '*he* does not see *himself* as *his* enemy'. Whether one reads this as 'Burgundy does not see himself as Charles' enemy' or 'Charles does not see himself as Burgundy's enemy', these lines give further evidence that Christine was aware of the negotiations taking place between Charles VII and Philippe le Bon. Cp. notes on ll.417–9 above.

ll.430–31. 'Nobody has the power to prevent him (Charles) from doing this i.e. entering Paris'.

LVI ll.443–5: the antecedent of *à qui* is *they* subject of *n'osent.*

l.446. *deservie* looks forward to and agrees with *punition.*

l.448. *maint.* When used as a collective noun, it may be given a plural verb as here.

LVII l.456. *don* i.e. the gift of forgiveness.

LVIII ll.457–8: *il* is impersonal in l.457; the subject of *retarde* l.458 is Charles VII understood. In reality, Charles' delay may have had as much to do with his own irresolution as with his reluctance to shed blood.

l.461. *qui rendre ne veult.* This is a standard idiomatic use of *qui* = 'if anyone'.

LIX l.467. Modern French would require a direct object to be stated. Cp. l.426.

BIBLIOGRAPHY

This bibliography includes only the manuscripts, texts and critical works referred to in our Introduction and Notes.

Manuscripts
Berne 205
Carpentras 390
Grenoble U.909. Rés.

Catalogues

Duhamel, M., *Catalogue général des manuscrits des Bibliothèques publiques de France. Départements. Tome XXXIV: Carpentras*, Plon, 1901.

Fournier, P., Maignien E., Prudhomme, A., *Catalogue général des manuscrits des Bibliothèques publiques de France. Départments. Tome VII: Grenoble*, Plon, 1889.

Hagen, H., *Catalogus codicum Bernensium (Bibliotheca Bongarsiana)*, Berne, Haller, MDCCCLXXIIII.

Lambert, C.G.A., *Catalogue descriptif et raisonné des manuscrits de la bibliothèque de Carpentras*, 3 tomes, Carpentras, E.Rolland, 1862.

Sinner, J.R., *Catalogus codicum MSS Bibliothecae Bernensis*, Berne, 1760–72.

Warner, G.F., and Gilson, J.P., *Catalogue of Western Manuscripts in the Old Royal and King's Collections*, British Museum, 4 vols. 1921.

On Language

Du Cange, *Glossarium mediae et infimae latinitatis*, 1884–7.

Godefroy, F. *Dictionnaire de l'ancienne langue française*, 1881–1902.

Pope, M.K. *From Latin to Modern French*, Manchester University Press, reprint of 1961.

Thesavrvs Lingvae Latinae, aditvs avctoritate et consilio academiarvm qvinqve Germanicarvm, Lipsiae, MDCCCC.

Tobler, A., and Lommatzsch, E., *Altfranzösisches Wörterbuch,* 1925–

Tobler, A. *Vermischte Beiträge* vol.1, Leipzig, Hirzel, 1921 ed.

Literary and Historical Texts

ALAIN CHARTIER, *The Poetical Works of Alain Chartier,* ed. J.C. Laidlaw, Cambridge University Press, 1974.

ANTONIO MOROSONI, *Chronique d'Antonio Morosoni,* ed. L. Dorez et G. Lefèvre-Pontalis, Paris, Renouard, 1898–1902, 4 vols., *Société de l'Histoire de France.*

BOKE OF NOBLESSE (THE), ed. J. Gough Nichols, London, Roxburghe Club, 1860.

CHRISTINE DE PISAN, *Avision-Christine,* ed. Sister Mary Louis Towner, The Catholic University of America Studies in Romance Languages and Literatures, vol. VI, originally published Washington D.C., 1932, reprinted by AMS Press, New York, 1969.

– *Ballades, Rondeaux et Virelais,* ed. Kenneth Varty, Leicester University Press, 1965.

– *Ditié de Jehanne d'Arc:* editions, partial editions in chronological order:

Jubinal, Achille, 'Ung beau Ditié fait par Christine de Pisan à la louange de Jeanne d'Arc', pp.75–88 of *Rapport à M.le Ministre de l'Instruction publique, suivi de quelques pièces inédites tirées des manuscrits de la Bibliothèque de Berne,* Paris, A la Librairie Spéciale des Sociétés Savantes, 1838.

Buchon, J.A.C., 'Documents divers sur Jeanne d'Arc', pp.540–3 of *Choix de chroniques et mémoires sur l'histoire de France avec notes et notices,* vol.XXXIV of the *Panthéon Littéraire,* Paris, A. Desrez, 1838.

Thomassy, Raymond, *Essai sur les écrits politiques de Christine de Pisan,* Paris, Debécourt, 1838, pp.XLII–XLVII.

Quicherat, Jules, 'Temoignages des Poëtes du XVe siècle Christine de Pisan, pp.3–21 of *Procès de condamnation et de réhabilitation de Jeanne d'Arc dite la Pucelle*, vol. 5, Paris, Renouard, 1849.

Herluison, H., *Jeanne d'Arc; chronique rimée*, Orléans, Herluison, 1865.

Le Roux de Lincy et L.M. Tisserand, 'Apostrophe de Christine de Pisan aux Parisiens dans 'Ung Beau Ditié fait l'an M.CCCC. XXIX' à la louange de Jeanne d'Arc', pp.420–7 of *Paris et ses historiens*, Paris, Imprimerie impériale, 1867.

Fabre, Joseph-Amant, 'Stances de Christine de Pisan sur Jeanne d'Arc', pp.307–330 of *Procès de réhabilitation de Jeanne d'Arc* 1888, republished Paris, Hachette, 1913, vol.2.

de Roche, Ch., and Wissler, G., 'Documents relatifs à Jeanne d'Arc et à son époque extraits d'un manuscrit du XVe siècle de la Bibliothèque de la ville de Berne' pp.329–52 of *Festschrift Louis Gauchat*, Aarau, 1926.

– *Epistles on the Romance of the Rose and other Documents in the Debate*, ed. Charles F.Ward, Chicago, 1911.

– *Epistre de la prison de vie humaine*, see S. Solente, 'Un traité inédit de Christine de Pisan', *Bibliothèque de l'Ecole des Chartes*, t. 85, 1924, pp.263–301.

– *Heures de contemplacion sur la Passion de Nostre Seigneur*, see S. Solente, 'Un traité inédit de Christine de Pisan' *Bibliothèque de l'Ecole des Chartes*, t. 85, 1924, pp.267–8.

– *Lamentacion sur les maux de la France*, pp.141–9 of R. Thomassy, *Essai sur les écrits politiques de Christine de Pisan*, Paris, Debécourt, 1838.

– *Lettre à Isabeau de Bavière* in *Anglo-Norman Letters and Petitions from All Souls MS. 182*, ed. M. Dominica Legge, Oxford, 1941, pp.144–50, *Anglo-Norman Text Society 3*.

– *Livre de la Cité des Dames*. For List of rubrics of B.N. ms. fr. 608, see Marie-Josèphe Pinet, *Christine de Pisan 1364–1430. Etude biographique et littéraire*, Paris, Champion, 1927, *Bibliothèque du XVe siècle* 35, pp.367–76.

– *Livre de la Mutacion de Fortune*, ed. S. Solente, Paris, Picard, 1959–1966, 4 vols., *Société des Anciens Textes Français*.

– *Livre de la Paix*, ed. Charity C. Willard, La Haye, Mouton, 1958.

– *Livre des fais et bonnes meurs du sage roy Charles V*, ed. S. Solente, Paris, Champion, 1936 and 1941, 2 vols. *Société de l'Histoire de France*.

– *Livre du Chemin de Long Estude*, ed. Robert Püschel, Berlin, Damköhler, Paris, Le Soudier, 1881 and 1887.

– *Livre du Corps de Policie*, ed. Robert H. Lucas, Genève, Droz, 1967, *Textes littéraires français* 145.

– *Oeuvres poétiques de Christine de Pisan*, ed. M.Roy, Paris, Firmin Didot, 1886–96, 3 vols., *Société des Anciens Textes Français*.

– *Sept Psaumes allegorisés*, ed. Ruth Ringland Rains, Washington, The Catholic University of America Press, 1965.

EUSTACHE DESCHAMPS, *Oeuvres Complètes* ed. Marquis de Queux de Saint-Hilaire et Gaston Raynaud, Paris, Firmin Didot, 1878–1903, *Société des Anciens Textes Français*.

JEAN FROISSART, *Oeuvres* ed. Kervyn de Lettenhove, Réimpression de l'édition de 1867–77, Osnabrück, Biblio Verlag, 1967.

JEAN JUVÉNAL DES URSINS, *Histoire de Charles VI* in Michaud et Poujoulat, *Nouvelle Collection de Mémoires relatifs à l'Histoire de France*, Paris, Didier, vol.2, 1857, pp.335–569.

PHILIPPE DE MEZIÈRES, *Le Songe du Vieil Pelerin*, ed. G.W. Coopland, Cambridge University Press, 2 vols., 1962.

PROCÈS DE CONDAMNATION ET DE REHABILITATION DE JEANNE D'ARC DITE LA PUCELLE, ed. Jules Quicherat, Paris, Renouard, 1841–49, 5 vols.

RELIGIEUX DE SAINT DENIS, *Chronique du Religieux de Saint Denis* in *Collection de Documents inédits sur l'histoire de France* 6, Paris, Crepelet, 1839.

STEPHEN SCROPE, translator, *The Epistle of Othea to Hector*, ed. G.F. Warner, London, Roxburghe Club, 1904.

Critical Studies

Chaume, M., 'Une prophétie relative à Charles VI', *Revue du Moyen Age Latin* iii, 1947, pp.27–42.

Delaunay, P., *La Zoologie au seizième siècle*, Paris, Hermann, 1962 (Histoire de la Pensée VII).

Du Castel, Françoise, *Damoiselle Christine de Pisan*, Paris, Picard, 1972.

Finkel, Helen Ruth, 'The Portrait of the Woman in the Works of Christine de Pisan' in *Les Bonnes Feuilles*, vol.iii, no.ii, Fall 1974, The Pennsylvania State University, pp.138–151.

France, Anatole, *Vie de Jeanne d'Arc*, Paris, Calmann-Lévy, ed. of 1924.

Grandeau, Y., 'Les Enfants de Charles VI', *Bulletin philologique et historique*, 1967, ii, pp.809–49.

Hamil, F.C., 'Presentment of Englishry and the Murder Fine', *Speculum*, XII, 1937, pp.285–298.

Howard de Walden, *Banners and Badges from a Tudor Manuscript in the College of Arms, The de Walden Library, London, 1904.*

Kennedy, Angus J., and Varty, Kenneth, '*Vernage*: Two Corrections to Godefroy', *Medium Aevum*, XLIV, 2, 1975, pp.162–3.

Laigle, Mathilde, *Le Livre des Trois Vertus*, Paris, Champion, 1912, *Bibliothèque du XVe siècle 16.*

Lang, Andrew, *The Maid of France*, London, Longmans Green, 1909.

Larnac, Jean, *Histoire de la littérature féminine en France*, 8e ed., 'Les documentaires', Editions KRA, Paris, n.d.

McLeod, Enid, *The Order of the Rose. The Life and Ideas of Christine de Pizan*, London, Chatto and Windus, 1976.

Migne, *Nouvelle Encyclopédie Théologique* vol. 24: *Dictionnaire des Prophéties et des Miracles*, 2 tomes, Paris, 1852.

Pernoud, Régine, *Joan of Arc*, Penguin Books, 1964.

– *La Libération d'Orléans*, Paris, Gallimard, 1969.

Pinet, Marie-Josèphe, *Christine de Pisan 1364–1430.* Etude *biographique et littéraire*, Paris, Champion, 1927, *Bibliothèque du XVe siècle 35.*

Potansky, Peter, *Der Streit um den Rosenroman* (Münchener Romanistische Arbeiten XXXIII), Munich, Fink, 1972.

Raknem, Ingvald, *Joan of Arc in History, Legend and Literature*, Universitetsforlaget, Oslo-Bergen-Tromsö, 1971.

Reeves, Marjorie, *The Influence of Prophecy in the Later Middle Ages. A Study in Joachimism.* Oxford, Clarendon Press, 1969.

Richardson, Lula McD., *The Forerunners of Feminism in French Literature of the Renaissance*, John Hopkins Studies in Romance Literatures and Languages vol. XII, Baltimore, 1929.

Rigaud, Rose, *Les idées féministes de Christine de Pisan*, Thèse présentée à la Faculté des Lettres de l'Université de Neuchâtel, Slatkine Reprints, 1973.

Robineau, E.M.D., *Christine de Pisan, sa vie et ses oeuvres*, Saint Omer, Fleury-Lemaire, 1882.

Sabatier, Robert, *La Poésie du Moyen Age*, Paris, A. Michel, 1975.

Solente, Suzanne, *Christine de Pisan. Extrait de L'Histoire littéraire de la France*, tome XL, Paris, Imprimerie nationale, 1969.

Vale, M.G.A., *Charles VII*, London, Eyre Methuen, 1974.

Vallet de Viriville, *Histoire de Charles VII et de son époque*, Paris, Renouard, 3 vols., 1862–5.

– 'Notes sur l'état civil des princes et des princesses nés de Charles VI et d'Isabeau de Bavière', *Bibliothèque de l'Ecole des Chartes*, 19, DIV, 1858, pp.473–482.

Wayman, Dorothy G., ,'The Chancellor and Jeanne d'Arc, February–July A.D. 1429', *Franciscan Studies*, XVII, 1957, pp.273–305.

GLOSSARY

The following abbreviations have been used: *adj.* adjective; *adv.* adverb; *cond.* conditional; *conj.* conjunction; *dem.* demonstrative; *f.* feminine; *fut.* future; *imperf.* imperfect; *indef.* indefinite; *indic.* indicative; *infin.* infinitive; *loc.* locution; *m.* masculine; *n.* noun; *p. hist.* past historic; *p.p.* past participle; *pers.* person; *pl.* plural; *prep.* preposition; *pres.* present; *pres. p.* present participle; *pron.* pronoun; *sing.* singular; *subj.* subjunctive; *v.* verb. An asterisk here and in the List of Proper Names indicates that the word is discussed in the Notes, Section II. Verbs are classified according to the forms which occur in the text.

abat 3 pers. sing. pres. indic. *abattre,* to strike down 312

abiles adj. able 285

accordance n.f. peace 436

acorde 3 pers. sing. pres. indic. *acorder,* to confirm, indicate 333

acquerre v. infin. to acquire, win 343

*adès** adv. now, at present; nevertheless 87

adhers p. p. *adherdre,* to be attached, joined to 362

adjouste 3 pers. sing. pres. indic. *adjouster,* to add 251

adonne 3 pers. sing. pres. indic. *adonner,* to bestow 351

*afflus** adj. bountiful 179

ainçois que conj. before 99–100, 237

ains adv. rather, on the contrary 276, 327

ains que conj. before 234, 340

ainsi que adv. as if 37

*aler, au long aler** loc. throughout history 203

amant pres. p. *amer,* to love 138

ame n.f. one single person, anyone; *sans le gref d'ame* to nobody's harm 131

amez p.p. *amer* to love 396

*ammonestoit** 3 pers. sing. imperf. indic. *ammonester,* to exhort, guide, counsel 215

amonition n.f. counsel, command 226

aplanié p.p. *aplanier,* to make smooth, peaceful 453

appareille 3 pers. sing. pres. indic. *s'appareiller à,* to compare with 204

apparu 3 pers. sing. p. hist. *apparoir,* to appear, become manifest 259

appelle 3 pers. sing. pres. indic. *appeler,* to invoke 254

appert 3 pers. sing. pres. indic. *apparoir,* to be evident 92, 216, 266; adj. evident 214

apreuve 3 pers. sing. pres. indic. *aprouver,* to approve 92

aprime 3 pers. sing. pres. indic. *aprismier,* to approach 36. See Notes Section I

arrestoit 3 pers. sing. imperf. indic. *arrester,* to stand firm 212

arroy n.m. array 43

assavourer v. infin. to taste, experience 317

asseurez p.p. *asseurer,* to reassure 398

assovye p.p. *assovir,* to bring to completion 344

*attendra** 3 pers. sing. fut. *attendre,* to wait; withstand, resist 419

aucuns pron. m. pl. some, some people 401, 485

aurés 2 pers. pl. fut. *avoir* 302

autrier n.m. the other day, a short time ago 309

avanture n.f. *se mettre à l'avanture contre,* expose oneself to 300

avenir v. infin. to come to pass, 73; n.m. used as adj. future 359

avenus p.p. *avenir,* to come to pass 156

aviengne 3 pers. sing. pres. subj. *avenir,* to happen, befall 366

avisement n.m. guidance 51

avises 2 pers. sing. pres. indic. *s'aviser,* to take stock, beware 438

avugle adj. blind 369

bel, par bel adv. with good grace 462

beneurée adj. blessed 161

benoist adj. blessed 170

bergiere n.f. shepherdess 198

bonement adv. happily 9

bonne adj. propitious 169

boute 3 pers. sing. pres. indic. *se bouter,* to enter 447

bouter v. infin. *bouter hors,* to cast, drive out 206

bugle adj. stupid 371

ça adv. here 373; *ça jus,* here below 351

cas n.m. fall; *flatir à cas,* overthrow, cast down 64

ce dem. pron. used as equivalent of modern French *ceci, cela* 280

*celle** dem. pron. f. *n'y ot celle,* there was no-one [who was not] 222 *cellui* dem. adj. m. that 126; dem. pron. 130

cens n. m. pl. hundreds 284

ceste dem. pron. f. this woman 205, 216, 346; dem. adj. this 224, 373

ceulx dem. pron. those men 451

ceulz dem. pron. those men 349

char n.f. flesh 459

chasteaulx n. m. pl. castles, fortified towns 282

chastel n.m. castle, fortified town 395

chenin adj. (from *chien*) wretched, base 267

chevetaine n.f. captain. leader 286

chief n.m. chief, ruler 478; author 120; *mettre à chief* v. infin. to complete 118

chiere n.f. face, expression 486

cil dem. pron. m. he, the person who 170, 341

cilz dem. pron. m. he 341

close p.p. *clore*, to enclose 2

com = *comme* 106 etc.

commise p.p. and adj. destined, ordained 240

compere 3 pers. sing. pres. indic. *comperer*, to pay 404

compte n.m. account; *fait grant compte,* 3 pers. sing. pres. indic. sets great store by 209

conclus p.p. *conclure*, to conclude, decide 328

conquerre v. infin. to conquer 341

conseil n.m. council 231

conseillié p.p. and adj. *conseillier,* to advise 433

consomé p.p. *consomer,* to accomplish 125

conte n.m. story, scripture 211

contralie 3 pers. sing. pres. indic. *contralier,* to oppose 403

contrariance n.f. opposition 437; adversity 148

contredire v. infin. to oppose, bar 410

contrediz n.m.pl. opponents 381, 414

convoiée p.p. *convoier,* to accompany 227

cornes n.f.pl. horns 305

courage n.m. heart, mind 473

courir sus, sur v. infin. to attack 68, 411; passive sense in 68 'being attacked'

creussent 3 pers. pl. imperf. subj. *croire,* to believe 272

croy 1 pers. sing. pres. indic. *croire,* to believe 424

cuidant pres. p. *cuidier,* to think, believe 410

cuident 3 pers. pl. pres. indic. *cuidier,* to think, believe 402

cuides 2 pers. sing. pres. indic. *cuidier,* to think, believe 427

cuidiés 2 pers. pl. imperf. indic. *cuidier,* to think, believe 313

cuidoit 3 pers. sing. imperf. indic. *cuidier,* to think, believe 105

debonnaire adj. good-natured, magnanimous 465

deboute 3 pers. sing. pres. indic. *debouter,* to reject 445

deceüz p.p. and n. the disappointed, disillusioned 63

defende 3 pers. sing. pres. subj. *defendre*, to prevent 428

deffault n.m. fault 404

degeté p.p. and adj. rejected 33

deprie 3 pers. sing. pres. indic. *deprier*, to invoke 254

derrain n.m. last, end 403

descombrant pres. p. *descombrer*, to clear out, expel 281

desert adj. ravaged, ruined 268; n.m. destruction 271 *mis à desert*, destroyed, exterminated

deservie p.p. *deservir*, to deserve 446

desliée p.p. *deslier*, to untie 164

desplace 3 pers. sing. pres. subj. *desplaire*, to displease 55

desplaist 3 pers. sing. pres. indic. *desplaire*, to displease 444

desur prep. above, in preference to 345

detrie 3 pers. sing. pres. indic. *detrier*, falter, go astray 256

deu n.m. due 144

deult 3 pers. sing. pres. indic. *(se) doloir*, to grieve 460

deust 3 pers. sing. imperf. subj. *devoir*, to have to, ought to 314

devant adv. before (of time) 272

devise 3 pers. sing. pres. indic. *deviser*, to speak about, discuss 331

dit n.m. word 255

ditié n.m. poem 481, *Explicit*

doint 3 pers. sing. pres. subj. *donner*, to give 52, 131

donné p.p. composed 481

doubt 1 pers. sing. pres. indic. *(se) doubter,* to fear 421

doubtance n.f. doubt 387

doubtans pres. p. *doubter,* to fear; fearful 400

doubter v. infin. to fear 147

douer v. infin. to bestow upon, endow with 168

droit n.m. the right 61; adj. clear, straight 20, *de droit oil* with a clear eye, clearly 20; adv. exactly 390

droiture n.f. right, justice 303

droiturier adj. upright 138

dueil 1 pers. sing. pres. indic. *(se) doloir,* to grieve over 23

dure 3 pers. sing. pres. indic. *durer,* to last, hold out 279; adj. resolute 277

effaciez p.p. *effacier,* to efface, erase 476

effusion n.f. shedding (of blood) 463

el pers. pron. she 246, 377

*election** n.f. choice; *sur toute election,* in preference to everything else 295

emblée n.f. surprise; *par emblée,* furtively, by stealth 411

embrunche adj. f. bowed, lowered, downcast 487

*enclose** p.p. and adj. enclosed 7

encoures adv. yet 132; still 418

*Englecherie** n.f. pejorative, the English race 354

*ennemis** n.m. sing. enemy 429

ennuiz n.m. troubles, difficulties 36

ens adv. inside 425, 428

ensercher v.infin. to find out, establish 236

ensuit 3 pers. sing. pres. indic. *ensuivre*, to follow 468

entens 1 pers. sing. pres. indic. *entendre*, to expect, believe 484; to understand, refer to, mean 441

envahis p.p. *envahir*, to attack 399

envoyez p.p. *envoyer*, to send, dispatch 415

erre n.m. or f. journey 340

*errerent** 3 pers. pl. p. hist. *errer*, to err 96

ert 3 pers. sing. imperf. indic. *estre*, 78, 258 (see also *yert*)

es contracted form *en* + *les*, in the 247

esbahir v. infin. *s'esbahir*, to be dismayed 65

esbaïs p.p. *s'esbahir*, to be dismayed 397

eschiquier n.m. chess-board 308; *matez estes en l'eschiquier*, you have been checkmated 308

escremie n.f. attack 421

escripz n.m. writings 244

esleu p.p. *eslire*, to elect 142

eslite adj. elect, chosen, blessed 184

espandre v. infin. to shed 460

esperit n.m. mind, mind's eye 243; *la virent en esperit*, foresaw her coming 242–3

espronné p.p. and adj. wearing spurs 40

esprouvée p.p. *esprouver*, to put to the test 230

esprouvez p.p. and adj. tried, trusty 289

essart n.m. clearing; *fera essart*, will destroy 337

essillié p.p. *essillier*, to lay waste 435

estat n.m. state, condition; house 94

estendre v. infin. to bestow 88

estroit adv. tightly 165

execution n.f. the carrying out (of a task) 290

eussent 3 pers. pl. imperf. subj. *avoir* 270

*face** 3 pers. sing. pres. subj. *faire* 252; 136*

faces 2 pers. sing. pres. subj. *faire* 144

faciez 2 pers. pl. pres. subj. *faire* 474

faillance n.f. failure; *sans faillance*, without fail 294

fais n.m. pl. deeds 147

*fait** n.m. achievement, deed 127, 140, 229, 248, 252, 352; situation 424*

faiz n.m. deeds 120, 178, 347; p.p. *faire* 71

fault 3 pers. sing. pres. indic. *falloir*, to be necessary 405, 412

feste n.f. celebration; *faisons feste à*, let us greet, welcome 41

feust 3 pers. sing. imperf. subj. *estre* 106, 439

fine adj. noble 39; 3 pers. sing. pres. indic. *finer*, to finish, end 483

finer v. infin. to finish, end 342

flati p.p. *flatir,* cast down; *flatir à cas,* to cast down, overthrow 64

fors prep. outside, beyond 274; *fors nature* supernatural 274

*fort** adj. strong 277; 39*

fort adv. greatly, extremely 220; *au fort* in the end 461

fouÿ 3 pers. sing. p. hist. *s'en fuir,* to flee 6

fu 3 pers. sing. p. hist. *estre* 283

fust 3 pers. sing. imperf. subj. *estre* 237

gaingne 3 pers. sing. pres. indic. *gaignier,* to win 304

gard 3 pers. sing. pres. subj. *garder,* to preserve 339

gardast 3 pers. sing. imperf. subj. *garder,* to prevent 431

gent n.f. people 191, 369

gisent 3 pers. pl. pres. indic. *gesir,* to lie 320

*grant** adj. great 88 etc.; 39*

gref n.m. harm; *sans le gref d'ame,* to nobody's harm 131

greigneur adj. comparative form of *grand*; supreme 478

grever v. infin. to harm 324

groingne 3 pers. sing. pres. subj. *groignier,* to grumble 425

guerdon n.m. reward, recompense 176

habonde 3 pers. sing. pres. indic. *habonder,* to abound 59

hait n.m. wish, desire, joy, aspiration 355

haÿs p.p. *haïr,* to hate 396

*herites** n.m. heretics 332

honnisse 3 pers. sing. pres. subj. *honnir* to shame, sully 140

*huer** v. infin. to shout 48

icellui dem. adj. m. that 98

incision n.f. incision, wound 459

infortune n.f. bad luck, misfortune 66

irés 2 pers. pl. fut. *aller* 316

ja adv. already 313

jus adv. down *ruer jus*, to cast down 78, 191, 195, 360; *ça jus*, here below 351

laboureur n.m. agricultural worker 210

laidit 3 pers. sing. pres. indic. *laidir*, to dishonour, treat with disrespect 336

largesse n.f. abundance 174

lassez p.p. and adj. wearied, tired 181

*lever** v. infin. to get up 325

lieva 3 pers. sing. p.hist. *se lever*, to rise up 37

lix n.m. lilies 96; 1 pers. sing. pres. indic. *lire*, to read 94

los n.m. praise 302

louez p.p. *louer*, to praise 293

mains adj. many 36, 223, 280, 389; *mains yeulx voiant*, in full view of everyone 280; *pou plus ou pou mains* adv. approximately 391; *le mains* n. the least 353

maint indef. pron. many, many a one 70, 196, 442, 448; adj. many a 127; 3 pers. sing. pres. indic. *manoir* to dwell, 72

mainte adj. f. many a 58

mais que conj. provided that 140, 144

manié p.p. *manier*, to handle, treat 455

maniere n.f. nature 248

matez p.p. *mater*, to mate (chess) 308

mecte 3 pers. sing. pres. subj. *mettre*, to put 473

menant pres.p. of *mener*; *menant joie*, rejoicing 46

menez 307, see *sornes*

menne 3 pers. sing. pres. indic. *mener*, to guide, lead 288

menra 3 pers. sing. fut. *mener*, to lead 339

menu adj. small 44

menus adj. small 157

mercy n.f. mercy, forgiveness 440

merveillable adj. astonishing, extraordinary 58

*mescreants** n.m. unbelievers 331

mesgnié[e] n.f. company, household 315

mie, ne . . . mie negative, not 418

mil n.m. one thousand 17, 482

miles n.m. thousands 284

mire n.m. doctor 412

*mission** n.f. mission 79

monstre 3 pers. sing. pres. indic. *monstrer*, to demonstrate 250

monstrent 3 pers. pl. pres. indic. *monstrer*, to demonstrate 347

monstriez 2 pers. pl. imperf. indic. *monstrer*, to demonstrate 310

*mors** adj. dead 263, 320, 374; *ne que mors chiens* no more than would dead dogs 263*

moult adv. much 444

muire 3 pers. sing. pres. subj. *mourir*, to die 340

muée p.p. *muer*, to change 80

ne negative conj. and, nor 212, 279, 375

neant n.m. nothing; *pour neant* in vain 405

norriture n.f. upbringing, education 276

notoire adj. well-known 82, 237

nul pron. nobody, not one 66, 279, 430

nulluy pron. anybody 472

nuit p.p. *nuire* to harm 70. See Notes Section I

occis n.m. the dead 325

occision m.f. killing, bloodshed 457

oit 3 pers. sing. pres. indic. *oïr*, to hear 323

onc. adv. ever; *onc* + *ne*, never 175, 199, 214–5, 260–1 *oncques* adv. ever; *oncques* + *ne*, never 95–6, 201–2, 379–80

or adv. now 13, 36 etc

orde adj. f. dirty, base, vile 332

ordonnée p.p. *ordonner*, to ordain 116, 171

ordonner v.infin. to dispose 468

ore adv. now 8

orent 3 pers. pl. p. hist. *avoir* 22

ores adv. now 24

orra 3 pers. sing. fut. *oïr*, to hear 471

os 1 pers. sing. pres. indic. *oser*, to dare 304

ose 1 pers. sing. pres. indic. *oser*, to dare 5

ot 3 pers. sing. p. hist. *avoir* 287, 381; *n'y ot celle*, there was no-one [who was not] 222

ou contracted form, *à* + *le*, 390; *en* + *le*, 302, 311; prep. (=*od*), with 389

*oultrance** n.f. excess 136

oultre prep. beyond; *oultre nature*, supernatural 192

oultrecuidance n.f. presumption 432

ouvré p.p. *ouvrer*, to work, act 112

ouÿ 3 pers. sing. p. hist. *oïr*, to hear 384

oÿ 1 pers. sing. p. hist. *oïr*, to hear 415

oÿez 2 pers. pl. imperative *oïr*, to hear 57

oÿsmes 1 pers. pl. p. hist. *oïr*, to hear 202

parfait p.p. *parfaire,* to bring to completion 350

part n.f. share 16

paru 3 pers. sing. p. hist. *paroir,* to appear, to be made clear 257

passeras 2 pers. sing. fut. *passer,* to surpass 139

passez adj. past 178, 345; *les preux passez,* brave men of times past 345

penon n.m. *pennon,* standard 103

perilleux adj. dangerous, fierce 310

pesans adj. heavy 275

peüst 3 pers. sing. imperf. subj. *povoir,* to be able 84

pevent 3 pers. pl. pres. indic. *povoir,* to be able 319

plain adv. in great numbers 381; adv. *à plain*, fully, entirely 383

plusers indef. pron. several 221

pou adv. little; *pou plus ou pou mains,* approximately 391; adj. and n. few 399

pourpris p.p. *pourprendre,* to undertake, accomplish 223

pourteroit 3 pers. sing. cond. *porter,* to bear 246

*premisse** n.f. first proof, manifestation 143

prens 1 pers. sing. pres. indic. *prendre* (*à*), to begin 8, 10

prensist 3 pers. sing. imperf. subj. (*en*) *prendre,* to befall, happen 100

*preuses** adj. brave 222*; 39*

*preux** adj. brave 199, 285; n.m. brave men 203, 345; 39*

pri 1 pers. sing. pres. indic. *prier,* to pray 51

prie 1 pers. sing. pres. indic. *prier*, to pray 130

*prime** n.f. prime (canonical hour) 37; *ore à prime*, for the first time, only now 8

prins p.p. *prendre* to capture 264

pris n.m. renown, worth 218; p.p. *prendre*, to capture 220

prophecies, propheciez n.f. prophecies 245, 124

propice adj. well-disposed, benign 141

provision n.f. relief, help 228

pry 1 pers. sing. pres. indic. *prier,* to pray 473

pueple n.m. people 141, 182, 220, 267;

puis prep. for, since 21; *puis . . . que* conj. since the time when 3–4; [*puis que*], because 109

quant (*des*) prep. as (for) 357

que conj. for 105

qui rel. pron. whoever 371, 403; if anyone 461

qui que rel. pron. whoever 55, 109, 357, 425

quoy, (*par*) *quoy* adv. phrase therefore, consequently 251; interrogative pron. (*se la chose n'yert. . .*) *evident quoy et comment* crystal-clear in every way 83

*quoy que** conj. although 409; indef. rel. pron. whatever 252; 215*

rabaissez 2 pers. pl. imperative *rabaisser*, to lower 305

raisonne 3 pers. sing. pres. indic. *raisonner,* to talk about 349

réa 3 pers. sing. p. hist. *reer*, to infuse, pour into 172 *regne* n.m. kingdom 268

regnié p.p. *regnier,* to disown, reject 450

relevée p.p. *relever,* to raise up 150

*relever** v. infin. to get up again 322

relieve 3 pers. sing. pres. indic. *relever,* to raise up 72

*remaint** 3 pers. sing. pres. indic. *remaindre,* to remain, hold out 396

rendre 3 pers. sing. pres. subj. *rendre,* to give, return 422

rendre v. infin. *rendre,* to surrender 405, 461

repassez p.p. *repasser,* to deliver 183

reprins p.p. *reprendre,* to reproach 472

reprint 3 pers. sing. p. hist. *reprendre,* to begin to 18

reprouver v. infin. to condemn 327

*repune** 3 pers. sing. pres. indic. *repugnier, repuner,* to oppose, resist 71

requerant pres. p. *requerir,* to request 454

requerir v. infin. to request 440

resjoïz p.p. and adj. rejoicing, overjoyed 43

respons 1 pers. sing. pres. indic. *(en) respondre,* to guarantee 443

restora 3 pers. sing. p. hist. *restorer,* to restore, deliver 219

retourné p.p. *retourner,* to change round, reverse; *si est bien le vers retourné,* the situation is completely changed 25

reusses 2 pers. sing. imperf. subj. *ravoir,* to have again, regain 108

revers n.m. opposite 364

rien n.f. thing, creature 31

rouppieux adj. base, vile 361

rué, ruée p.p. of *ruer jus*, to cast down 195, 360, 78

ruer jus v. infin. to cast down 191

sacre n.m. anointing 377

sacré p.p. *sacrer*, to anoint 384

sauf et sains adv. safely and soundly 388

sçay 1 pers. sing. pres. indic. *sçavior*, to know 417

se conj. if 5, 59 etc.

*sec** adj. dry, barren (season) 32

secourable adj. helpful, willing to help 60

sejour n.m. stay; *fu à sejour*, resided 392

sensible adj. intelligent 111

serés 2 pers. pl. fut. *estre* 472

serfs n.m. serfs, slaves 365

sermonner, v. infin. to speak, hold forth 471

si and, and yet 305, 353 etc; *si com* as 143, 260; *si que* just as 422; *si que* so that 479

solempnée adj. solemn 117

somé p.p. *somer*, to call, appoint 127

somme n.f. quantity 194; *toute somme*, in short after all 197

sornes n.f. jokes; *ne menez voz sornes*, do not attempt any foolish, rash enterprise 307

soubz prep. under 103, 478

soubzmis p.p. *soubzmettre*, to subjugate 103

souffers p.p. *souffrir*, to tolerate 367

souffisance (à) adv. sufficiently 146

souffise 3 pers. sing. pres. subj. *souffire*, to suffice 375

souffrir v. infin. to tolerate, put up with 327

souffrant pres. p. *souffrir*, to suffer, endure 35

souloie 1 pers. sing. imperfect indic. *souloir*, to be wont to 11

sours p.p. *sourdre*, to rise up 269

souviengne 3 pers. sing. pres. subj. *souvenir*, to remember 368

soyes 2 pers. sing. pres. subj. *estre* 153

*sué** p.p. *suer; il en est sué*, it is all up with them (?) 358

suppliance n.f. supplication 439

surnommé p.p. *surnommer*, to name, designate as 124

sus, *courir sus* to attack 68; passive sense 'being attacked' 68

tabourer v. infin. to beat a drum 316

tart (à) late i.e. not at all, never 456

*tel** adj. 113 etc; 39*

*telement** adv. 262; 39*

tendra 3 pers. sing. fut *se tendre*, to hold out, resist 417

tendre adj. young 86

tendront 3 pers. pl. fut. *se tenir*, to consider oneself 485

tenir v. infin. *(me)tenir*, to confine (myself) 12

tenu p.p. *tenir,* to hold back 45

tenuz p.p.and adj. obliged, under an obligation to 154

tiens 1 pers. sing. pres. indic. *tenir,* to maintain, hold 260

tire, de tire adv. directly 6; *tire à tire* adv. phrase one by one 413

tira 3 pers. sing. p. hist. *tirer,* lead out of, deliver 181

*tirée** p.p. (se) *tirer* de, to move from 32

tors n.m. wrongs, evil deeds 71

tramise p.p. *trametre,* to send 238, 373

*tresgrande** adj. 39

trespasse 1 pers. sing. pres. subj. *trespasser,* to leave out, omit 52

[*tres*]*tous* adj. all 139

treuve 3 pers. sing. pres. indic. *trouver,* to find 93

trop adv. of intensity, much 439

une adj. f. constant 69

univers adj. universal, whole 57

vaillance n.f. courage 296

valable adj. valuable, of profit 63

vault 3 pers. sing. pres. indic. *valoir,* to be of account, to be worth 402

véa 3 pers. sing. p. hist. *veer,* to refuse 175

véez 2 pers. pl. imperative *voir,* to see 192

veille 3 pers. sing. pres. indic. *veiller (à)*, strive to 205

vendrez 2 pers. pl. fut. *venir*, to come 456

*vers** prep. towards 37*; n.m. situation 25

vesqu p.p. *vivre*, to live 22

veult 3 pers. sing. pres. indic. *voloir*, to wish 323, 326, 461

veulx 1 pers. sing. pres. indic. *voloir*, to wish 24

vises 2 pers. sing. pres. indic. *viser*, to think, reflect; *mal y vises* you are quite miscalculating 440

voir adj. true 401

voire adj. true 87

voirement adv. truly 81

voix n.f. voice; *par voix commune*, unanimously 68

voiz n.f. voices 323; 2 pers. sing. imperative *voir*, to see 101

vueil 1 pers. sing. pres. indic. *voloir*, to wish 49

vueillent 3 pers. pl. pres. subj. *voloir*, to wish 406

vueillez 2 pers. pl. imperative *voloir*, to wish 469

yert 3 pers. sing. imperf. indic. *estre* 82 (see also *ert*)

*yvernage** adj. wintry 10

LIST OF PROPER NAMES

www.ingramcontent.com/pod-product-compliance
Lightning Source LLC
Chambersburg PA
CBHW030119170426
43198CB00009B/670